THE
WORD
AND THE
SPIRIT

Paul Cain

R. T. Kendall

CREATION HOUSE

THE WORD AND THE SPIRIT by Paul Cain and R. T. Kendall
Published by Creation House
A part of Strang Communications Company
600 Rinehart Road
Lake Mary, Florida 32746
www.creationhouse.com

Unless otherwise noted, all Scripture quotations are from
the New International Version. Copyright © 1973, 1978,
1984, International Bible Society. Used by permission.

Scripture quotations marked KJV are from the King
James Version of the Bible.

Scripture quotations marked NAS are from the New
American Standard Bible. Copyright © 1960, 1962, 1963,
1968, 1971, 1972, 1973, 1975, 1977 by the Lockman
Foundation. Used by permission.

Library of Congress Cataloging-in-Publication Data
Cain, Paul.
The Word and the Spirit / Paul Cain, R. T. Kendall.—
1st U.S. ed.
    p. cm.
    ISBN: 0-88419-544-9 (paperback)
    1. Bible—Evidences, authority, etc.—Congresses. 2. Word
of God (Theology)—Congresses. 3. Holy Spirit—Congresses.
I. Kendall, R. T. II. Title.
BS480.C27 1998
231'.3—dc21   98-27452
                                                              CIP

This book previously published by Kingsway Publications,
Eastbourne, E. Sussex, copyright © 1996,
ISBN: 0-85476-413-5.

0 1 2 3 4 5 6 BBG 8 7 6 5 4 3 2
Printed in the United States of America

"The church needs to go through a genetic code change. That is what this book is about, and that is why it is important."

—GERALD COATES
PIONEER

"The emphasis of this book on both Word and Spirit is refreshing and welcome."

—TONY SARGENT
WORTHING TABERNACLE

"It was the great church elder Tertullian who said in the third century A.D. that the two hands of God the Father were the Word and the Spirit. I applaud R. T. Kendall and Paul Cain for their partnership in bringing these two hands together. At last we are beginning to understand what Tertullian meant."

—J. JOHN
EVANGELIST

To every church leader committed to the remarriage of the Word and the Spirit.

Acknowledgments

I want to thank my friends at Beulah for all they did for us at that first Word and Spirit Conference. They are lovely, godly people, and we thank God for them.

My warm thanks to Kingsway Publications for their unending patience with us in getting this book published in Great Britain. And thanks to the Creation House staff for their efforts in publishing this in America.

I thank Lyndon for his hard work behind the scenes, among which was joining me in asking Graham to write his wonderful hymn. Thank you, Graham and Jill, for your encouragement, and thank you, Graham, for putting the thoughts together that summarize the theme of this book and for writing the hymn.

Contents

But I would bring everything to the test of the Word and the Spirit. Not the Word only, but the Word and the Spirit. "God is a spirit," said our Lord, "and they that worship Him must worship Him in Spirit and in truth."

While it is never possible to have the Spirit without at least some measure of truth, it is, unfortunately, possible to have a shell of truth without the Spirit. Our hope is that we may have both the Spirit and the truth in fuller measure.

—A. W. TOZER, THE DIVINE CONQUEST

PREFACE

THIS BOOK IS made up of the six addresses that Paul Cain and I gave at the Wembley Conference Centre in London in October 1992. The conference was sponsored and organized by Beulah, an interdenominational group of churches in North London. Lyndon Bowring chaired the meetings, and Graham Kendrick led the worship at the evening celebration. He introduced his hymn "Jesus, Restore to Us Again," written for the occasion, which centers on the need for the Word and the Spirit to come together in the church.

Minimal editing has been done to these messages. This is especially the case with the fifth address, "A

Post-Charismatic Era." It was not intended to be an expository sermon but rather a statement. The apostle Paul gave an allegory about Hagar and Ishmael and Sarah and Isaac. (See Galatians 4:21–31.) He did this in the context of showing the place of the Law. What I have done with the original story is to apply it prophetically to our day.

I believe that ancient history is repeating itself. As Abraham sincerely thought that Ishmael was the promised son, so many have believed that the Pentecostal/Charismatic movement was the revival God promised. It is my view that Isaac is coming, a work of God greater than anything heretofore seen—even in proportion to Isaac's greatness over Ishmael.

Paul Cain and I first met in October 1990 when he spoke at the London Arena. He had earlier prophesied "tokens of revival" concerning these meetings. I myself was one of those "tokens!" I have not been the same since. I too had been hasty. I had actually warned prominent church leaders against this man whom I felt was occultic. Like so many, I was more ready to believe in the devil's power than in the power of God. I had to change my mind. It was not the first time I had to climb down, nor was it to be the last! Paul is now a member of Westminster Chapel. His impact on us has been vast and timely.

Some have wryly noted that our ministries at Wembley represented a "role reversal." Paul was to have represented the "Spirit" side; I was "Word." But he turned out to emphasize the Word more and I the prophetic. This was not planned, but perhaps this too has some prophetic significance: Those who have been largely into "signs and wonders" may turn out equally to be great exponents of the Word, and those of us who have been largely limited to biblical exposition may one day move into the power of the Spirit as well.

Paul and I firmly believe the church is on the brink of a post-charismatic era of unprecedented glory. He prophesied in March 1993, "Isaac will be an ugly baby." He went on to say that at first "Isaac will look like Ishmael." He will "burp like Ishmael, need diapers changed like Ishmael." But as an ugly baby can turn out to be a most beautiful person, so Isaac will be the "most handsome child that ever was."

—R. T. Kendall

INTRODUCTION

by Colin Dye

WHAT GOD HAS joined together, let man not separate" (Matt. 19:6). With these words Jesus gave the most comprehensive affirmation ever spoken about the binding nature of the covenant of marriage. But there is another "marriage made in heaven," which is also firmly rooted in God's revelation: the union of the Word and the Spirit. Like the union between a man and a woman, this "marriage" is frequently threatened by passing trends and fashions. It seems that one viewpoint is almost always asserted to the detriment of the other. To hold to both equally is, as church history has proven, an intensely difficult and elusive challenge that few have attained. And yet, as in the human marriage experience, the two are made for each other and cannot truly be complete without each other.

The division often wedged between the Word of God and the Holy Spirit is unnatural and forced. All Scripture is God-breathed, that is, the breath of God's lips, His Word. It carries the very breath, or Spirit, of God. This is why Jesus was able to say, "The words I have spoken to you are spirit and they are life" (John 6:63). God always works through His Word and His Spirit. Both are active executors of His will. God's Word spoken is His promise fulfilled, and the Spirit acts to bring it about.

All this makes the current discussion in evangelical and charismatic circles very interesting. Instinctively we are seeking to bring together into mainstream Christian experience the correct balance and harmony between the Word and the Spirit. It is biblically incorrect to speak about the two in separation, but it is also plainly apparent that in our experience the two are not getting along as they should. Too often churches are known for the one or the other. Either a church is strong in the Word and doctrine, or it is renowned as a place of spiritual manifestation. This is not how it should be. Jesus was known as a "prophet, powerful in word and deed before God and all the people" (Luke 24:19). The early church stood strong in doctrine and in the power of the Lord. And so must we.

That is why the Word and the Spirit Conference was and (now with these published papers) is so important. The conference came out of an unlikely friendship between two men who, when they first met, recognized in each other what was missing in their own experience and knowledge of God. R. T. Kendall said to Paul Cain, "I need your power," and the other replied, "I need your theology!"

That they should ever work together in Christian ministry is even more surprising, considering that they each came from what some would consider to be opposite ends of the Christian spectrum. One is evangelical and reformed by persuasion, and the other is charismatic and pentecostal by experience. Paul Cain is well known for the strong measure of supernatural manifestation that accompanies his ministry, particularly in the areas of healing and the prophetic, while Dr. R. T. Kendall is one of the foremost Bible teachers and theological exponents of our age.

I was at the conference in Wembley, and I was personally encouraged by what these two men were doing and saying. Some were disappointed, failing to look beyond the immediate occasion that was, by some estimations, only an "average" conference. However, many like myself were personally edified by the teaching and encouraged by the prophetic direction given through the event. The Lord even gave me a personal word of prophecy through Paul Cain, which encouraged me to press for the freedom I needed within my pentecostal denomination to develop the work of church planting from my church in London, Kensington Temple.

Dr. Kendall's statement about a "post-charismatic" era caused quite a stir. Some non-Charismatics present were offended by the affirmation he gave to the Charismatic movement, while some Charismatics were offended at being compared to Ishmael! And yet the future of the church depends on our learning from each other. I personally look forward to the day when we will no longer have to argue the case for the so-called Charismatic movement as its benefits will be completely accepted into the mainstream. That I believe is the biblical position. However, every charismatic leader I know is looking for the greater move of God to come.

This century has been perhaps the most remarkable century in Christian history. The pentecostal revivals, at the beginning, set the pace for the phenomenal church growth in many places for the rest of the century. The nonwestern world has hosted continuous revival in one part or another since then, and today over one hundred thousand people worldwide come to faith in Christ daily. With the arrival of the Charismatic Renewal in the 1960s, the movement spread until every denomination in the West was also affected. It is estimated that up to six hundred million people living in the world today have a pentecostal or charismatic experience. Dr. Peter Wagner calls this the most remarkable growth of any nonmilitary movement in history.

But it is not enough. Twenty-five percent of the world's population is culturally and geographically excluded from the gospel. The western world is being described as post-Christian. And the developing world is crippled by debt, disease, and political turmoil. Non-Christian religions are having their own "revivals." It is clear we need something more than we have witnessed. Nothing short of a revival of full-blooded apostolic Christianity will turn the tide and enable us to rise to the challenge of the twenty-first century. The Pentecostal and Charismatic movements, as great as they have been, simply cannot be all that God has for us. The way forward must, in the first instance, take us back to the apostolic truths and the apostolic power by which they were experienced, lived out, and proclaimed to a dying world.

The time came when the greatest obstacle to the fulfilment of Isaac was the presence of Ishmael. Up to that time, Ishmael was the closest thing on earth to the fulfillment of God's promise to Abraham, but he was not the promise. R. T. Kendall and Paul Cain challenge us to learn from the experience of God's Spirit through the Charismatic movement while not holding on to it as if it were all that God wants to do in our lifetime. The message of the conference is even more clear to us today than it was at the time of the conference, helped by the startling spiritual events in numerous nations over the past several years. These appear to many to be an indication of a new move of God's Spirit that could well take us on into a new era of revival. If we heed the message of this book, this revival may prove to be the long awaited "Isaac"—the church of power and purity, of the Word and the Spirit.

That same day the Sadducees, who say there is no resurrection, came to him with a question. "Teacher," they said, "Moses told us that if a man dies without having children, his brother must marry the widow and have children for him. Now there were seven brothers among us. The first one married and died, and since he had no children, he left his wife to his brother. The same thing happened to the second and third brother, right on down to the seventh. Finally, the woman died. Now then, at the resurrection, whose wife will she be of the seven, since all of them were married to her?"

Jesus replied, "You are in error because you do not know the Scriptures or the power of God. At the resurrection people will neither marry nor be given in marriage; they will be like the angels in heaven. But about the resurrection of the dead—have you not read what God said to you, 'I am the God of Abraham, the God of Isaac, and the God of Jacob'? He is not the God of the dead but of the living."

When the crowds heard this, they were astonished at his teaching.

—MATTHEW 22:23–33

One

THE REMARRIAGE OF THE WORD AND THE SPIRIT

by R. T. Kendall

I WANT TO LOOK at this passage in Matthew where the Sadducees came to Jesus with their biases and prejudices, and then I want to look at the response Jesus gave and see how this relates to our theme, "Word and Spirit." I want to deal in the main with verse 29: Jesus said to the Sadducees, "You are in error because you do not know the Scriptures or the power of God."

THE SCRIPTURES AND THE POWER OF GOD

WE BEGIN WITH verse 33: "When the crowds heard this, they were astonished at his teaching." I am fascinated that Jesus' teaching could bring about such an emotion. They were *astonished* at His teaching. It's the same word used in Matthew 7:28–29 when, at the end of the Sermon on the Mount, the crowds were "amazed at his teaching, because he taught as one who had authority, and not as their teachers of the law." It's the same word used in Luke 9:43 when Jesus cast out a demon; everyone was "astonished." It's the word used in Acts 3:10 after a forty-year-old man, lame from birth, was instantaneously, miraculously healed—all were "astonished."

I think of Graham Kendrick's hymn, "Restore, O Lord, the Honor of Your Name." How do you suppose the restoration of that honor is to come about? Some might say that it will only come through a demonstration of signs, wonders, and miracles. That could be true. But I believe that God is going to withhold the phenomena of signs and wonders from the church generally until two things coalesce: the Scriptures and the power of God; the Word and the Spirit. For example, in 1 Thessalonians 1:5 the apostle Paul said, "Our gospel came to you not simply with words, but also with power, with the Holy Spirit and with deep conviction." Paul said to the Corinthians in 1 Corinthians 2:4: "My message and my preaching were not with wise and persuasive words, but with a demonstration of the Spirit's power." He combined the Scriptures with a demonstration of the power of God: the Word of God and the Spirit of God. Another way of putting it, as we shall see later, is to say that the Word and the name of God will be remarried.

But Jesus' way of putting it in our text is the combination of the Scriptures and the power of God. The

2

word for *power* is the same as the word used in Luke 24:49 when Jesus said, "Stay in the city until you have been clothed with power from on high." It's the word used in Acts 1:8: "You will receive power when the Holy Spirit comes on you." The two together—the Scriptures and the power of God—are the only explanation of what happened when Peter preached on the day of Pentecost.

We must be clear by what we mean by "Scriptures." We mean the Bible, God's inerrant and infallible Word. By "power" we mean a supernatural force that has no natural explanation. Only God could do it.

Jesus said that the Sadducees were ignorant of both of these. Now with some people it has been one or the other. There are those who are well acquainted with the Scriptures. They know their Bibles. They know their doctrine. They even know their church history. They can detect heresy a mile away.

And there are those who are well acquainted with the raw power of God. They have experienced the infilling of the Holy Spirit. They have experienced His gifts. They have seen healings, even miracles. And they can detect dead orthodoxy a mile away.

There is wrong with either emphasis—each is exactly right. Take, for an example, those of us who represent the Reformed tradition as I do. We say, "We must earnestly contend for the faith once delivered unto the saints. We must recover our Reformation heritage. We must return to the God of Jonathan Edwards and Spurgeon. We must be sound in doctrine."

Or take another example, those who come from a pentecostal or charismatic perspective. They say, "We must recover apostolic power. The need of the day is for a renewal of the gifts of the Spirit. Signs and wonders were seen in the Book of Acts; we too must see them. What is needed is a demonstration of power."

My message to you today is this. The church generally will struggle on and on in its plea for God to restore the honor of His name until it is not one or the other, but both—the Scriptures and the power of God.

Here are two things we ought to know. Here are two things the Sadducees didn't know. Here are two things that must be emphasized. And here are two things that ought to be experienced simultaneously.

The Sadducees were descended largely from priestly families. They traced their ancestry back to the priest Zadok, from whom their name is derived. They were the aristocracy of the day, fewer in number than the Pharisees but far more influential. The Sadducees knew it all. You know the illustration: You can always tell an Oxford man, but you can't tell him much! Well, that was the Sadducees. They didn't think—they *knew* they were the experts on the Law of Moses. They had minimal respect for the prophetic. Their authority was the Pentateuch, the first five books of the Bible. To them the prophets of the Old Testament were second class.

According to Acts 23:8, their main doctrinal distinctives were: (1) no resurrection of the body; (2) no angels; (3) no such thing as disembodied spirits—they felt that the soul died with the body; they were annihilationists. They despised Jesus of Nazareth. That the Pharisees felt the same way about Jesus wasn't enough to win the Sadducees over. For the Sadducees were determined to prove two things: that their doctrinal distinctives were correct, and that

Jesus was to be ignored as a phenomenon that would soon pass.

In the dialogue between Jesus and the Sadducees in Matthew 22:23–32, the Sadducees were very proud of themselves for having come up with an airtight case that would prove their point and put Jesus in His place. "'Teacher,' they said, 'Moses told us that if a man dies without having children, his brother must marry the widow and have children for him.'" They followed this legal statement with an illustration. No doubt they made it up. It was theoretically possible, but in any case it suited their purpose. They asserted: "'There were seven brothers among us. The first one married and died, and since he had no children, he left his wife to his brother. The same thing happened to the second and third brother, right on down to the seventh. Finally, the woman died. Now then, at the resurrection, whose wife will she be of the seven, since all of them were married to her?'"

Jesus was not intimidated by their attempt to ensnare Him. His reply was, "You are in error." William Hendriksen translated it this way: "You are deceived, for you do not know the Scriptures or the power of God." What a thing to say to those who think they know everything! How many of us have the honesty and integrity and enough objectivity about ourselves to see it and admit it if we have been deceived? In this case, their deception and unteachable spirit sprang from ignorance. Jesus said, "You do not know." Jesus is using the Greek word *ginosko,* which is often used to show what has been revealed. That's the way some people know things: by revelation. He uses another word, *oidate,* which often means "knowledge of a well-known fact." He said, "You're ignorant—you're not even acquainted with that for which you think you're an expert."

Fancy this! Saying to the Sadducees, experts in the Pentateuch, "You are ignorant of the Scriptures." Could you imagine saying that to a seminary professor, or to an Oxford don, or a New Testament scholar? And yet I ask, "Could it possibly be true of us?" I have a deep-seated fear that Christians today don't know their Bibles. The time was, even in this century, when ordinary Christians knew their Bibles. One person could quote a part of a verse and another could finish it and tell you exactly where it is located. Today many church leaders can't even do that.

Then Jesus added, "You're not only ignorant of the Scriptures; you are equally ignorant of God's power." Now why bring that up? They weren't the slightest bit interested in that subject. They had not come to talk about God's power; that was the furthest thing from their minds. It was Jesus who brought it up. Nothing was more irrelevant to them. I wonder how many today are like that. You have felt that your knowledge of Scripture was enough, that your emphasis upon doctrine was enough. You felt that this is really what matters and that talk of God's power was for the apostolic era only.

The church today, generally speaking, is like the pharaoh "who did not know about Joseph" (Exod. 1:8). Joseph, prime minister of Egypt, had made the children of Israel heroes in Egypt. The fat of the land was theirs. The pharaoh of that time gave them everything they wanted. But that pharaoh died. In the meantime, the children of Israel grew and multiplied. The new pharaoh felt threatened by the growing number of Israelites, and he did not know about

Joseph who had also died. The new pharaoh persecuted the children of Israel. It was as though there never had been a Joseph.

The church today is like that, perhaps a million pharaohs "who know not Joseph." There are those who aspire to do God's work but don't know His Word. It is said that Luther and Calvin gave us the Word in the sixteenth century, but this is the twentieth century, and God wants us to do the works. But we don't know the Word. We are pharaohs who seem to owe nothing to our historic past.

In John 14:26, Jesus said that one of the things the Holy Spirit would do would be to bring to our remembrance what we had been taught. Whenever you read that verse about the Holy Spirit, don't forget that Jesus' disciples had been trained. They were taught, they'd heard a lot, they'd learned a lot. Would they forget what they had learned? "Don't worry about that," said Jesus. "The Holy Spirit will bring to your minds what you learned."

I hear a lot of people talking about the desire to be Spirit filled, and I applaud that desire. But I have to tell you that if you are empty-headed before you are Spirit filled you will be empty-headed after you are Spirit filled, because there'll be nothing there for the Spirit to remind you of. I believe that revival is coming—an unprecedented kind of outpouring such as was seen in Jonathan Edwards' day, unlike anything our generation has seen. The question is, Are we ready for it? Have we been trained? Have we been taught? God will use most those who have sought His face, not His hand, who have searched His Word and stood in awe of it.

Job could say, "I have treasured the words of his

mouth more than my daily bread" (Job 23:12). The psalmist could say, "I have hidden your word in my heart that I might not sin against you" (Ps. 119:11). How many of us memorize Scripture—an art that has virtually perished from the earth? You ask, "What's the use? Why read the Bible? Why memorize Scripture? Why endure teaching? It is so boring; it is so un-inspiring."

I answer, "One day it will pay off; the Spirit will bring to your mind what you've learned."

THE WORD AND THE NAME

THIS AWAKENING, which I believe is coming, will come when the Scriptures and the power of God come to-gether. Another way of putting it, as I said earlier, is that the Word and the name of God are rejoined—remarried. The two ways God unveiled Himself in the Old Testament were through His Word and His name. "I will bow down toward your holy temple and will praise your name for your love and your faithfulness, for you have exalted above all things your name and your word" (Ps. 138:2). The King James Version actually got it right; it reads, "Thou hast magnified thy word above all thy name."

What is the Word? It is what came to Abraham, Isaac, and Jacob. It is what Abraham believed and so was saved. "Abraham believed the LORD, and he credited it to him as righteousness" (Gen. 15:6). It's the way people are saved still.

> But what does it say? "The word is near you; it is in your mouth and in your heart," that is, the word of faith we are proclaiming: that if you

8

confess with your mouth, "Jesus is Lord," and believe in your heart that God raised him from the dead, you will be saved.

—ROMANS 10:8–9

What about the name? It was first disclosed to Moses. It says in Exodus 3:6 (the very verse that Jesus quotes to the Sadducees), "'I am the God of your father, the God of Abraham, the God of Isaac and the God of Jacob.' At this, Moses hid his face, because he was afraid to look at God." But listen to Exodus 6:2–3: "God also said to Moses, 'I am the LORD. I appeared to Abraham, to Isaac and to Jacob as God Almighty, but by my name the LORD I did not make myself known to them.'"

How could this be? Abraham, Isaac, and Jacob knew and responded to the Word of God, but they did not know His name. How is it possible? The answer is, because for us God's Word has priority over His name. We are saved by the hearing of the Word. That is how God made Himself known to Abraham. That's how Abraham was saved; that's how we are saved.

This explains how it is possible for a church to continue without signs and wonders. We are not saved by signs and wonders. We're saved by a gospel that tells us Jesus died on the cross for our sins and rose from the dead. Hearing that Word of grace and embracing it by faith is what saves us. This is why we will go to heaven when we die and not to hell. The blood that Jesus shed on the cross of Calvary two thousand years ago is the most precious commodity in the history of mankind. The blood that dripped from His hands, from His feet, and from His head cried out to God, and it satisfied the justice of God. By it we are saved; without it we are lost. It is hearing that Word that brings us from death to life.

People can see signs and wonders and go to hell. People can experience signs and wonders and go to hell. People can minister signs and wonders and go to hell. Jesus said, "Many will say to me on that day, 'Lord, Lord, did we not prophesy in your name, and in your name drive out demons and perform many miracles?' Then [Jesus] will tell them plainly, 'I never knew you. Away from me, you evildoers!'" (Matt. 7:22–23).

Having said that, remember that it is also possible to know the Word and be lost. It is possible to be sound in doctrine and never be converted. There are people who sit under the ministry of preaching, and you discover, to your astonishment, that they have never been converted. So don't say that just because you're sound in doctrine you're going to heaven. You can be sound in doctrine and be lost. The devil believes and trembles.

Make no mistake, the gospel of Jesus Christ is complete without signs and wonders. But the Bible is not complete without signs and wonders.

One day God appeared to Moses. Moses got up that morning not knowing that this day would be different. He was watching sheep at the foot of Mount Horeb. He saw a bush on fire. Perhaps there was nothing unusual about that; he'd seen it before. But he noticed that this time there was something different; the bush didn't burn up. One of two things would be true. Either the bush was different or the fire was different. And he began to look more closely.

Many want what Moses wanted. He wanted a rational explanation for what was happening. We all have our questions. Some things are too deep to be revealed this side of eternity. God said simply, "Stop. Take off your shoes. You are on holy ground." (See Exodus 3:5.) And in that event, an event through which Moses would never again be the same, God unveiled His name—"I AM WHO I AM" (v. 14). He went on to say that He revealed Himself to Abraham, Isaac, and Jacob as *God Almighty,* but He didn't reveal His name to them.

Unprecedented phenomena accompanied the unveiling of God's name—signs and wonders. It began with the burning bush. It continued with Aaron's rod, which was turned into a serpent. It continued on with the ten plagues of Egypt, culminating with the night of Passover and the crossing of the Red Sea on dry ground. The revelation of God's name was inaugurated with an unprecedented kind of power. There were signs and wonders that defied a natural explanation.

How do we summarize the relationship of Word and name? The Word relates to God's integrity: His promise, His grace, His inability to tell a lie. It is the way we are saved. The name relates to His honor, His reputation, His power, and His influence. So while God's Word refers to His integrity, His name refers to His vindication.

But the Sadducees knew about neither. "You are in error," said Jesus, "because you do not know the Scriptures or the power of God." They didn't even know what Exodus 3:6 really meant—that the issue behind that verse was the honor of God. What happened to Abraham, Isaac, and Jacob? Were they just

11

relics of the past? Did they die like dogs or cattle or trees? Jesus gave the Sadducees the shock of their lives. He turned their smug interpretation on its heels and with it not only affirmed the resurrection of the dead, but of angels and immortality of the soul as well—the existence of an intermediate state demands the resurrection of the body. He said to them in verse 30, "At the resurrection people will neither marry nor be given in marriage; they will be like the angels in heaven." *Resurrection* means "the end of death." There will be no need for the procreation of the race. We will be like the angels in heaven.

At this point Jesus said, as it were, "Oh, by the way, about the resurrection of the dead, have you not read what God said to you, 'I am the God of Abraham, the God of Isaac, and the God of Jacob'? He is not the God of the dead but of the living." In other words, Abraham, Isaac, and Jacob are alive and well. They are in heaven right now with the angels. Their souls are with God. Their disembodied spirits are with God. They are at this moment with the Lord and worshiping him.

HOW TO OBTAIN POWER

CONTAINED IN THESE verses is basis for power, power in the right sense. At the natural level, and often in the wrong sense, we all want power. This is why people want a pay raise. This is why people want a promotion. In 1960 they asked John F. Kennedy, "Why do you want to be president of the United States?"

He said, "Because that's where the power is."

In a spiritual dimension, we should be greedy for power. Jesus said, "Stay in the city until you have been clothed with power from on high...You will receive power when the Holy Spirit comes on you" (Luke 24:49; Acts 1:8). The apostle Paul warned us against "having a form of godliness but denying its power" (2 Tim. 3:5).

What then is the basis for God's giving spiritual power to His followers? I identify four aspects.

1. PERSONAL READING OF THE SCRIPTURES

It is almost humorous to read what Jesus said to the Sadducees: "About the resurrection of the dead—have you not read?" (Matt. 22:31). Nevertheless we have to ask ourselves a question: "Have I read my Bible? Have I read it completely through?" There are those who think, *Well, I need to read my Bible today. Let's see—Psalm 115, I'll read that today.* They have no plan, no plans even to have a plan. Jesus would say to you, "You don't know the Scriptures."

Would you be afraid to have how much you read your Bible and how much you pray flashed on a giant screen for everybody to see? A recent poll was taken suggesting that the average clergyman in Britain spends an average of four minutes a day alone with the Lord. Do you wonder why the church is powerless? Martin Luther once said, "I've got a very busy day. I must spend not two but three hours in prayer." Personal reading of the Scriptures is the first step to power.

2. PERSONAL REVELATION OF THE SCRIPTURES

Notice how Jesus put it. "Have you not read what God said to you?" (Matt. 22:31). In other words, Jesus said, "It's for you, Sadducees."

But if it was for the Sadducees it would be for anybody. If it could be true for the skeptical, sure, smug Sadducees, it is true for anybody. God originally said it to Moses, but Jesus said, "It's for you." *It's for us—* personal revelation, when God's Word gets hold of you. You want the prophetic word, don't you? When is the last time the Scriptures got hold of you and shook revelation knowledge into your life? Spurgeon said, "If a text gets hold of you, chances are you've got hold of it." When is the last time that God's Spirit went right through you like a laser beam when you were reading your Bible?

3. PERSONAL RETHINKING OF THE SCRIPTURES

Do you know that the words of Exodus 3:6, "I am...the God of Abraham...Isaac and...Jacob," were as well known to the Sadducees as John 3:16 is to us? Jesus said, "Have you not read Exodus 3:6?" How would you feel if somebody said to you, "Have you not read John 3:16?"

You might say, "You're not serious!"

You can hear the biting sarcasm in Jesus' words: "Have you not read what God said to you?" Of course you couldn't have told the Sadducees anything about Exodus 3:6. That was ABC. To them it merely meant, "We worship the same God in our day as they worshiped in their day." Jesus said, "Wrong, you missed it. You missed the real meaning altogether. What it means is that Abraham, Isaac, and Jacob are alive. God is not the God of the dead but of the living." And the Sadducees were devastated.

Many of us are locked into a point of view with

regard to certain Bible verses or teaching, just like the Sadducees. We know it all. We have accepted un-critically a hand-me-down point of view, secondhand Bible revelation, and secondhand doctrine. "So-and-so believes it; I believe it. It was taught me. I've always believed it this way." There is no personal rethinking by which we acquire the real meaning of the verse.

4. PERSONAL RELEASE OF THE SPIRIT

Release of the Spirit comes from the Spirit Himself. The question is, How are you going to get on good terms with the Spirit? If you want power, it's going to have to come from the Spirit. If you want to get on good terms with the Spirit, then get on good terms with His book. The Bible is just about His finest accomplishment. It's His product. He likes it when you like His Word. Do you say that you love the Holy Spirit? He's saying to you today, "Do you? Really?" A release of the Spirit will result in a personal renewal of power that will restore the honor of God's name.

Forgive me if I'm wrong, but my suspicion is that when it comes to the theme "Word and Spirit," many of us are more interested in the Spirit than we are in the Word. Some readers may be very disappointed to find that the preponderant emphasis in this book is on the Word. Note verse 33 of Matthew 22: "When the crowds heard this, they were astonished...." At what? At signs and wonders? At a demon being exorcised? A lame man being healed? No. "They were astonished at his teaching." It was the teaching that did it, Jesus' exposition of Exodus 3:6—a verse familiar to any Sadducee.

I fear that we have so lost confidence in the authority of the Word that it has hardly crossed our minds to determine what power is contained in the Word to astonish. Jesus could astonish with the Word as easily as He could with signs and wonders. You will say, "Well, if I could have Jesus giving me the exposition all the time, I too would be astonished."

I answer, "You have the greatest expositor with you. He is in you: the Holy Spirit." The Spirit will be released to the degree that we stand in awe of His Word.

The scope for power will be found to the degree that we value His own Word. Signs following will be His seal on us. Power that flows from His name will be in proportion to our love for His Word. When that love is expressed, don't be surprised to see healings and miracles, signs and wonders come during the preaching of the gospel. There may be no need for people to line up to be prayed for. It will happen right where they are.

The man for whom I was named, my father's favorite preacher, who went by his initials, Dr. R. T. Williams, used to say to young ministers, "Young men, honor the blood and honor the Holy Ghost." By that he meant that the word of the gospel should emphasize Jesus' blood and that the Holy Spirit should be in control of the services we lead. We can never upstage the gospel. But we must be open to the Spirit.

I fear a silent divorce has taken place between the Word and the Spirit, between the Word and the name, between the Scriptures and the power of God. When there is a divorce, some children stay with one parent, some side with the other.

In our day there are those who line up behind the emphasis upon the Word. Others say, "I want to see power." There are those who come to our services expecting to hear the Word, and all the time I hear, "Dr. Kendall, thank you for your word. It was a good word." The Word is what they wanted, and that's what they got. Others want to see a demonstration of power. They want to see things happen.

When these two—the Word and power—are brought back together, a remarriage occurs and the simultaneous combination will mean a spontaneous combustion. The day will come—I believe sooner than we think—when those who come to see will hear, and those who come to hear will see.

In the beginning was the Word, and the Word was with God, and the Word was God. He was with God in the beginning.

Through him all things were made; without him nothing was made that has been made. In him was life, and that life was the light of men. The light shines in the darkness, but the darkness has not understood it.

There came a man who was sent from God; his name was John. He came as a witness to testify concerning that light, so that through him all men might believe. He himself was not the light; he came only as a witness to the light. The true light that gives light to every man was coming into the world.

He was in the world, and though the world was made through him, the world did not recognize him. He came to that which was his own, but his own did not receive him. Yet to all who received him, to those who believed in his name, he gave the right to become children of God—children born not of natural descent, nor of human decision or a husband's will, but born of God.

The Word became flesh and made his dwelling among us. We have seen his glory, the glory of the One and Only, who came from the Father, full of grace and truth.

—JOHN 1:1–14

Two

THE ROLE OF THE WORD

by Paul Cain

I AM VERY EXCITED about the theme of this book, the Word and the Spirit. I believe they are the two edges of the selfsame sword. Obviously Dr. Kendall's ministry is more known for his expository preaching—the exposition of the Word of God— whereas my little ministry is better known for some expressions of the Spirit now and then.

However, we desperately need both the Word and the Spirit. Dr. Kendall and I agree that God wants to bring about a divine remarriage of the power of the Word and the power of the Spirit. There are questions that we are not able to answer as yet. Let's not presume that we have all the answers. But we are asking some questions, and leaving it to you to find some answers.

Before we look at the role of the Word, I want to address a subject that I believe is a vital theme for today. I feel that we must take a serious look at the subject of *unity*.

THE NEED FOR UNITY

FIRST OF ALL, I believe that we need unity because of the direct correlation between unity and the anointing. Psalm 133:1–2 says:

> How good and pleasant it is when brothers live together in unity! It is like precious oil poured on the head, running down on the beard, running down on Aaron's beard, down upon the collar of his robes.

There is another reason why we need unity: One can chase a thousand; two can set ten thousand to flight. (See Deuteronomy 32:30.) Just that wonderful part of Scripture alone makes me want to go for unity.

It is our unity that will convince an unbelieving world of the reality of Jesus Christ and His church. I believe this unity must be evident to an unbelieving world—and not just evident in heaven. In John 17:21, Jesus prayed that we may be one. And then He continued on to say why: "So that the world may believe that you have sent me." We have an awesome task to perform—"Word" people and "Spirit" people need a remarriage to convince the world that we're one, and we'll never achieve unity just through signs and wonders alone. (See John 15:24.) That would be completely out of balance. Jesus said, "By this all men will know that you are my disciples, if you love one another" (John 13:35). We need love and unity to convince this world of the reality of Jesus Christ and His church.

When the world sees the church in unity, there is a greater hope that it will believe. I'm not talking about ecumenical unity, but unity of the Spirit. Therefore in considering unity, we're not talking about mindless and spineless abandonment of essentials of the faith that form the very backbone of Christianity, doctrines such as the deity of Christ, the inerrancy and sufficiency of Scripture, and justification by faith. We must have true unity, and to have it will require a walk in humility.

In James 4:6 we are reminded that God resists the proud, but He gives His grace to the humble. Ephesians 4:2–3 commands us to "be completely humble and gentle; be patient, bearing with one another in love. Make every effort to keep the unity of the Spirit through the bond of peace."

So the issue of unity is directly related to the whole concept of the remarriage of the Word and the Spirit. We must come to grips with the fact that those in the body of Christ have a desperate need for each other. We cannot fulfill God's purpose alone (as 1 Corinthians 12:20–27 makes very clear).

THE PREEMINENCE OF THE BIBLE

LET'S LOOK AT the role of the Word of God in the light of Joshua's encounter with the Lord after the death of Moses. Apparently Joshua was more than eighty years old at this time when the Lord commanded him:

> Do not let this Book of the Law depart from your mouth; meditate on it day and night, so that you may be careful to do everything written in it. Then you will be prosperous and successful.
>
> —JOSHUA 1:8

Joshua had no doubt been an ardent student of the Law for decades, yet here he is, eighty years old, still walking in the Word after all this time—charged by God to meditate on the Word day and night. You can't imagine how this makes me feel; this Scripture has deeply challenged me since I knelt at the foot of the cross so many years ago at the age of eight. I am well into my sixties now, yet the call of God to love His Word and meditate therein day and night has never been more precious to me than now. It's never been more urgent; this call of God for all believers to get back to His Word is more vital than we have realized. If we want the blessing and the approval of God that Joshua experienced, then we need to get back to the Bible. It is our true foundation of faith and practice, and we must meditate in His Word day and night. God will show up.

Despite the winds of controversy that are blowing today, I want to say emphatically that I believe there are no new revelations. There are just fresh revelations of old truths. I believe it is impossible to overstate the importance of believing in the infallibility of the Word of God, that is, the infallibility of the Bible. If you are a church leader, and you betray the slightest doubt about the infallibility of the Bible, what do you suppose your church members will do? When we talk about the Word and the Spirit, let no one doubt what we mean—we mean the Bible is affirmed and made alive by the Holy Ghost. By the Bible we mean the Old Testament as well as the New. We do well to remember that Jesus never apologized for the Old Testament.

When the church had its optimum level of power, whether on the day of Pentecost (Acts 2:2) or that day when the place was shaken (Acts 4:31), they categorically affirmed the Old Testament. So conscious was the apostle Paul of being under divine inspiration that he said to the church at Corinth in 1 Corinthians 14:37, "If anybody thinks he is a prophet or spiritually gifted, let him acknowledge that what I am writing to you is the Lord's command." Simon Peter not only said that the Old Testament was written by men who "spoke from God as they were carried along by the Holy Spirit" (2 Pet. 1:21), but he equated the writings of the apostle Paul with the same authority as he did the writings of the Old Testament Scripture:

> He writes the same way in all his letters, speaking in them of these matters. His letters contain some things that are hard to understand, which ignorant and unstable people distort, as they do the other Scriptures, to their own destruction.
>
> —2 PETER 3:16

The greatest folly that we could impose on this generation is to let them think they can improve upon the Word of God.

The Word speaks of the futility of putting a new patch on an old garment (Matt. 9:16; Luke 5:36; Mark

2:21). We cannot dress up the Word of God and make it better or more palatable. Such an attempt merely distracts from the Word of God.

When we get more excited about a prophetic word than we do about the written Word, we show how little we think of the Bible. I remember the lady in my charismatic church setting who, although very proper and very nice, upset me by continually asking me to give her a word from the Lord. One day she came up to me and said, "Mr. Cain, do you have a word from the Lord for me?"

This time she pushed me over the edge. Holding up a Bible, I said, "Oh, yes, dear lady. Here is a whole book of them! Take this and read it for yourself."

Well, as dramatic as that was, she thought I was under the anointing, and she took the Bible, read it, and became a walking Bible. I saw her a year later in Arizona, and she was aflame, aglow. She was the head of the Women's Aglow! It was wonderful.

We must love the God of the Bible, and we must know the God of the Bible. Could it be that the main reason we're not seeing more signs and wonders today is because we're more interested in them than we are in the written Word?

Hundreds of times in our evangelistic ministry I have found something that really works: "It is written" really works. When you begin to build on the Word of God, speaking the Word as it is written, the Holy Spirit comes alongside, and you will experience what we call "the anointing." I'm prepared to prophesy that the more we become excited about the Word of God, the more power we will see. We don't need just the power of demonstration; we need the demonstration of power, and I'm expecting the Lord to honor His Word by His Spirit.

I believe that we're not going to be able to penetrate this radical culture in which we live unless we have a radical commitment to the Word of God. Jesus described the enemy that would try to thwart the Word of God.

> The worries of this life, the deceitfulness of wealth and the desires for other things come in and choke the word, making it unfruitful.
> —MARK 4:19

Many Christians today are unfruitful because the enemy has used the deceitfulness of wealth and materialism and the desire for other things to choke out the Word of God in their lives.

There are times when the right kind of prosperity can come your way, and it's a blessing. There's a time when we would call it "the ugly head of prosperity" that would take you from the Word of God and from the purposes of God in your life.

Like Jesus in the wilderness when Satan was tempting Him, we must depend on nothing less than "It is written" at a time like that. I often wondered why Jesus didn't perform some great miracle; He could have called the angels to dance behind Him. He could have put on a tremendous show, but He did something that every one of us can do any day of our lives—at any given time we can say, "It is written." And I want to let you in on a little secret: The only way I've survived this long in the ministry is to preface a precious promise of God, an applicable pertinent promise, with "It is written." I've done this thousands of times.

It is written…"It is God who arms me with strength and makes my way perfect" (Ps. 18:32).

It is written…"When I am afraid, I will trust in you" (Ps. 56:3).

According to some scholars there are seven thousand such promises in Scripture—so remembering them ought to keep us busy until the power comes!

Someone may say, "Well, I tried that, and it didn't work."

I will respond, "Did you try it until you died? Keep on trying."

In Matthew 4:4, Jesus said, "Man does not live on bread alone, but on every word that comes from the mouth of God." If we're going to be a prophetic church that can impact the culture in which we live in a relevant way, we need a radical agenda. I heard Baptist pastor Steve Gaukroger say, "Radical does not mean out with the old and in with the new; radical does mean out with the old, and in with the even older—that is, the Bible, the Word of God."

The Bible is the most radical agenda that has ever been. It goes back to where God's truth is stated so clearly. I believe the church will shake the nations only when we have a radical commitment to *all* the Bible, not just our favorite parts and the Scriptures with which we feel comfortable. The Bible genuinely must be what we believe and what we follow.

> For the word of God is living and active. Sharper than any double-edged sword, it penetrates even to dividing soul and spirit, joints and marrow; it judges the thoughts and attitudes of the heart.
>
> —HEBREWS 4:12

THE NEED FOR THE SPIRIT

I AM STAGGERED by the number of people who see a contradiction between a commitment to Scripture and a commitment to the Spirit. I cannot see this distinction in the Bible, where we are constantly reminded of the absolute necessity of the Holy Spirit being in active leadership in every phase and facet of the church—including the decision-making process—as well as in our individual lives.

As Romans 8:14 says, "Those who are led by the Spirit of God are sons of God." We need to remember that Jesus did not say to His disciples. "It's better that I go away so that I can send you a book!" He said, "It's better for you that I go away so that I can send you the Holy Spirit."

An Episcopal rector one day shocked all Americans who were listening to *The Episcopal Hour* with a statement that's often quoted: "If the Holy Spirit were withdrawn from the church today, 90 percent of the church would go right on as though nothing had happened."

So it is Word and Spirit we need. We cannot overestimate the importance of meditating in the Word day and night, and embracing all of the Bible, no matter with whom it identifies us and no matter from whom it separates us. Yet nor should we continue to confuse the role of the Holy Spirit, either by downplaying what He does or by overstating what He does. We must gain a fresh commitment to unity if we want the great anointing, or the greater anointing, that God has promised to release to His church in these last days. We must have unity. We must see our need for each other. We need good theology, and we need the power of God.

I want to say as emphatically as I know how: In the next move of God there are no superstars. We are all begotten by the Word; we are tested by the Word; and we are to be governed by the Word.

In a vision a few years ago, it seemed I could see the Lord standing as He stood before Joshua. In His hand He held the sword of God. I said, "O Lord, whose side are You on?"

And He said, "I have not come to take sides; I have come to take over."

"No eye has seen, no ear has heard, no mind has conceived what God has prepared for those who love him"—but God has revealed it to us by his Spirit.

The Spirit searches all things, even the deep things of God. For who among men knows the thoughts of a man except the man's spirit within him? In the same way no one knows the thoughts of God except the Spirit of God. We have not received the spirit of the world but the Spirit who is from God, that we may understand what God has freely given us. This is what we speak, not in words taught us by human wisdom but in words taught by the Spirit, expressing spiritual truths in spiritual words. The man without the Spirit does not accept the things that come from the Spirit of God, for they are foolishness to him, and he cannot understand them, because they are spiritually discerned. The spiritual man makes judgments about all things, but he himself is not subject to any man's judgment: "For who has known the mind of the Lord that he may instruct him?"

But we have the mind of Christ.

—1 CORINTHIANS 2:9–16

Three

THE ROLE OF THE SPIRIT

by Paul Cain

I N THE LAST chapter we considered the theme of
the Word and the necessity of unity. Now we
look more closely at the role of the Spirit.

Britain has produced some of the greatest preachers
the world has ever known, and many of these have
prophetic elements in their ministries, often without
knowing it. I believe that Charles Spurgeon had the
word of knowledge operating clearly and distinctly
in his preaching ministry. I may be hard pressed to
prove this, but I've been told that recent research has
uncovered some of the wonderful things that these
men of God of past generations have had in terms of
prophetic input.

Prophetic preaching of the Word is something that's on the agenda for the next move of God, and prophetic preaching in a culturally relevant way is as powerful a gift as anyone with the "word of knowledge," as it is called. I believe the key to preparing the way for revival will come through dynamic prophetic preaching, and we're well on our way to that.

I want to discuss some of the attributes of the Holy Spirit that are found in the Bible, but I also want to stress the necessity of the Holy Spirit's being the leader of our lives. I look forward to the day when the decision-making process of the church engages the Holy Spirit in every board meeting, and those meetings would be less boring! We need the Holy Spirit to guide us, to direct us, to lead us, and to teach us.

THE SPIRIT OF TRUTH

ONE OF THE most striking things about the Holy Spirit is found in the Gospel of John, where He is called "the Spirit of truth" (John 14:17; 15:26; 16:13). Can you imagine having the Holy Spirit functioning in you to the point that you could tell when someone is preaching the truth and when someone is preaching false doctrine? That's what the Holy Spirit of truth is all about.

THE TRUTH ABOUT GOD

THE FIRST REASON He is the "Spirit of truth" is because He reveals to us the truth about God. When God comes on the scene the Holy Spirit automatically accompanies Him and tells the truth about God. The Father, Son, and Spirit are "glory-dumpers." Have you ever noticed that Jesus dumps the glory on the Father, and then the Father dumps the glory on the Son, and the Holy Spirit dumps the glory? We might learn a lesson from Him; He comes to magnify the Lord Jesus Christ. We need to magnify and exalt the name of the Lord Jesus.

I hope the day will soon come when, because of His marvelous acts and His power to save and heal and deliver to the uttermost, the name of Jesus Christ will be made more famous than it was in A.D. 33. The world needs to see our unity and our love for one another, for Jesus said, "By this all men will know that you are my disciples, if you love one another"—and *then* the Lord will give us the power of His Spirit. "He made known his ways to Moses, his deeds to the people of Israel" (Ps. 103:7). Don't take for granted that you can know the ways of God just because you read the Bible. Moses' prayer in Exodus 33:13 was, "Teach me your ways." It takes the Spirit of truth to reveal to us the heart of God; that's what the Lord does when, through the Holy Spirit, He shows us what He hates and how much He hates it, what He loves and how much He loves it. For instance, God hates pride. Proverbs 16:18 says, "Pride goes before destruction, a haughty spirit before a fall." Pride is the sin that we see in everybody else but never in ourselves unless we allow the Holy Spirit to reveal it to us. It is possible to read the Bible every day of our lives and still not see our pride. What good is it if we can discourse profoundly on the Trinity and then grieve the persons of the holy Trinity?

It not only takes the Holy Spirit to know what God hates, but also it takes the Holy Spirit to know what

He loves. We must find out what God hates—and hates with a passion—and not do those things any more. And we must find out what God loves and love it with all of our hearts.

What does God love? We can do worse than begin with those words of the prophet Micah:

> He has showed you, O man, what is good. And what does the LORD require of you? To act justly and to love mercy and to walk humbly with your God.
>
> —MICAH 6:8

You can only learn humility by the Spirit. It cannot be grasped intellectually; it comes by revelation, by the Holy Spirit.

THE TRUTH ABOUT US

SECONDLY, THE Holy Spirit not only reveals the truth about God, but He reveals the truth about ourselves. Many churches would welcome the Holy Spirit today if it were not for the fact that the Spirit of truth is liable to reveal any sin or pride or ambition—anything that is not of God. Any unholy fear and unrighteousness will be revealed.

"The heart is deceitful above all things and beyond cure. Who can understand it?" (Jer. 17:9). We cannot even know the sin of our own hearts apart from the ministry of the Holy Spirit—the Spirit of truth. When the Holy Spirit strips off all our false façade and self-righteousness, we're left naked, open, and shameful before all. "When he comes, he will convict the world of guilt in regard to sin and

34

righteousness and judgment" (John 16:8). Our darkened heart is one of the primary reasons that we must have the Holy Spirit of truth—we can't trust ourselves. I'm not in favor of all of this self-help today—pulling oneself up by one's own bootstraps. We need the Holy Spirit to expose us and explore us and reveal the secrets of our hearts.

THE SPIRIT OF INTERPRETATION

THE HOLY SPIRIT wrote the Bible, therefore it makes sense that He's the best interpreter of it. In John 14:16–17 the Holy Spirit is called "the helper" in the New American Standard Bible, our "comforter" in the King James Version, and our "counselor" in the New International Version. Jesus says that the Holy Spirit must be our teacher (John 14:26). He "will teach you all things and will remind you of everything I have said to you." We need the Holy Spirit more than we may realize. It is "'not by might nor by power, but by my Spirit,' says the LORD Almighty" (Zech. 4:6).

THE SPIRIT OF REVELATION

AS THE PASSAGE of Scripture at the beginning of this chapter makes clear, we can't see or hear anything from God apart from the supernatural revelation of the Holy Spirit (1 Cor. 2:9–16).

THE SPIRIT OF TESTIMONY

THE SPIRIT ALSO bears testimony; He witnesses to Jesus and empowers us to do the same. The Holy Spirit "will testify about me" (John 15:26).

But you will receive power when the Holy Spirit comes on you; and you will be my witnesses in Jerusalem, and in all Judea and Samaria, and to the ends of the earth.

—ACTS 1:8

After they prayed, the place where they were meeting was shaken. And they were all filled with the Holy Spirit and spoke the word of God boldly.

—ACTS 4:31

THE SPIRIT OF GLORY

ANOTHER PRIMARY ROLE of the Holy Spirit, as we have seen, is to glorify Jesus. No one can bring glory to God apart from the Holy Spirit. "He will bring glory to me by taking from what is mine and making it known to you" (John 16:14). The Spirit uncovers the glory of Jesus to us. In Ephesians 1:17–20, the apostle Paul prayed:

That the God of our Lord Jesus Christ, the glorious Father, may give you the Spirit of wisdom and revelation, so that you may know him better. I pray also that the eyes of your heart may be enlightened in order that you may know the hope to which he has called you, the riches of his glorious inheritance in the saints, and his incomparably great power for us who believe. That power is like the working of his mighty strength, which he exerted in Christ when he raised him from the dead and seated him at his right hand in the heavenly realms.

THE SPIRIT OF LOVE

THE SPIRIT REVEALS the nature of God's love for us. Paul states that "God has poured out his love into our hearts by the Holy Spirit, whom he has given us" (Rom. 5:5). Paul describes God's love in greater detail in his prayers for the Ephesians:

> I pray that out of his glorious riches he may strengthen you with power through his Spirit in your inner being, so that Christ may dwell in your hearts through faith. And I pray that you, being rooted and established in love, may have power, together with all the saints, to grasp how wide and long and high and deep is the love of Christ, and to know this love that surpasses knowledge—that you may be filled to the measure of all the fullness of God.
>
> —EPHESIANS 3:16–19

THE UNITY OF THE SPIRIT

IT TAKES THE Spirit to lead us to unity when we differ. Philippians 3:15 says, "All of us who are mature should take such a view of things. And if on some point you think differently, that too God will make clear to you."

I've experienced God's clarification many times, which comes when we allow the Holy Spirit to correct us. It is a divine necessity to be open to the Holy Spirit for correction if we want unity. None of us have all the answers; someone said it is nothing short of chronological snobbery to think that we in the twentieth century have got it right and everybody else has got it wrong. If we will be patient God will bring us to unity.

GRIEVING THE SPIRIT

EVERYTHING JESUS told us about the Holy Spirit is subject to one thing: that He, the Holy Spirit, be allowed to be Himself. He wants to be Himself in us—that is, to be ungrieved. John the Baptist was told that "the man on whom you see the Spirit come down and remain is he who will baptize with the Holy Spirit" (John 1:33). I would say that I have lived through several expressions of revival, and I have seen the Spirit descend a number of times, but He did not remain. He does not remain when He is grieved, and it is our duty to see which way the Lord is moving and not grieve the Holy Spirit when He comes. He needs to be allowed to be Himself in us.

We grieve the Holy Spirit by our pride. Our pride is expressed in various ways:

> And do not grieve the Holy Spirit of God, with whom you were sealed for the day of redemption. Get rid of all bitterness, rage and anger, brawling and slander, along with every form of malice.
>
> —EPHESIANS 4:30–31

When I hold a grudge against a brother, I have already grieved the Holy Spirit. I should not be surprised if the Bible is not real to me any longer and no longer comes alive when I read it. I'm sure that a grudge has opened the door to depression for more people than we realize.

38

Elijah became depressed because he was angry with the Lord and felt betrayed by Him. He had a grudge against God. It is often no different for us. "Elijah was a man just like us" (James 5:17)—and he found himself with a grudge, and that grudge opened the door to depression strong enough for him to wish he were dead! He didn't go so far as to want to kill himself, but he asked God to do it for him.

We open the door to depression when we harbor a long-standing grudge. I wish we could just dump all of our grievances and grudges and bitterness; all of this clamor and evil-speaking and malice would be put away and done in. That kind of deliverance would usher in the greatest miracle service we could ever hope for.

The spirit of rivalry grieves the Holy Spirit. "Honor one another above yourselves" (Rom. 12:10). I want to say this again: There will be no superstars in the next movement. What could possibly grieve the Holy Spirit more than denominational rivalry and the spirit of competition among churches, robbing Peter to pay Paul? We grieve the Holy Spirit by refusing to be self-effacing. The greatest liberty we can possibly have may result.

I don't have many luxuries—I enjoy my privacy, but more than anything else I also enjoy the freedom of having nothing to prove. I don't like the bondage of having to come to a spiritual meeting under the stress of having to perform, or of calling people out of the audience, or of looking like some kind of a prophet. The greatest freedom that I could possibly enjoy is standing up and saying, "I have nothing to prove, I just want to lift up the Lord Jesus Christ and glorify Him by the help of the Holy Spirit. I want to make Jesus look as good as He possibly can look; I want to decrease and let Him increase."

Why do we need to tell people that they should follow us instead of somebody else, or that we have it right? We should have a carefulness about us, never wanting to draw disciples to ourselves. That very thought frightens me, and I don't think I could possibly hope to live very long if I had an attitude that I'm drawing disciples to myself. I wouldn't know what to do with them after they were drawn, so that's not in the picture. What is this need that some may have of getting our name in headlines? It is because of this deeper need to prove that we are right.

Some church leaders have marriages that are falling apart because they care more about being right, more about proving something than they do about their marriage relationships. Often their spouses can't stand them...their marriages are on the rocks. The Lord wants to heal them. To be healed, they need to become vulnerable to one another and start loving their partners. I know I'm a celibate and I'm not supposed to know about this, but I believe Jeremiah was an unmarried man, and Paul also (despite what some theologians say). These two men knew more about family life, marriage, raising children, inner peace, inner happiness, and inner animation than anyone else in the Bible as far as I'm concerned. So I am convinced that marriages can be healed today if we could just overcome this desire to be proven right all the time.

I saw this illustrated some time ago through a conversation with a friend. He came in to my office one day, beaming. I said, "How are you today?"

And he said, "Oh, I'm great!"

And I said, "No, you're not."

He said, "What?"

He had just had a fight with his wife—and thought that he had won. But the Holy Spirit, the Spirit of truth, was coming alongside. "No, you're not doing all right," I said. "Brother, demeanor is everything."

He said, "What do you mean?"

I explained, "*De-longer* you talked to your wife a while ago, *de-meaner* you got!"

He said, "How did you know that? I thought I'd won!"

We must become vulnerable; if you become vulnerable in your marriage, the Lord will heal that marriage. Love "keeps no record of wrongs" (1 Cor. 13:5). A vindictive spirit grieves the Holy Spirit.

Why do we need to put down our brother just so he appears less credible? Why do we compete with God and not let God do the work that He does best, namely vindication? "It is mine to avenge; I will repay" (Deut. 32:35; cf. Rom. 12:19).

How dare we say that we want a demonstration of the Spirit when we ourselves have grieved Him by our own bitterness, spirit of rivalry, boasting, name dropping, and destroying one another's credibility? There are no shortcuts to power. Don't talk to me about being slain in the Spirit—talk to me about your pride being slain.

THE SPIRIT OF POWER

IN CONCLUSION, we need the Spirit to come in power. We must never forget that the kingdom of God consists in power, not in words, as Paul reminds us in 1 Corinthians 4:20: "For the kingdom of God is not a matter of talk but of power." So much of our

Christianity today consists of talk only.

We need to beware of the signs of ungodliness, which Timothy warned would mark the last days. In 2 Timothy 3:5 and 7, Paul warns us of two of the perils of the last-day church: "Having a form of godliness but denying its power…always learning but never able to acknowledge the truth." Are you denying the power of God? I hope they are not speaking of any of us.

This was true of so much of the orthodox religious establishment of Jesus' day; that is why Jesus said, "You are in error because you do not know the Scriptures or the power of God" (Matt. 22:29). It is possible to be religious and orthodox in theology and moral authority and not know the Word of God at all. In fact, this is exactly what happens when you exclude the Holy Spirit from the church.

Jesus rebuked the Sadducees and Pharisees and the orthodox religious leaders of His day:

> And the Father who sent me has himself testified concerning me. You have never heard his voice nor seen his form, nor does his word dwell in you, for you do not believe the one he sent. You diligently study the Scriptures because you think that by them you possess eternal life. These are the Scriptures that testify about me, yet you refuse to come to me to have life.
>
> —JOHN 5:37–40

A religious spirit is one that glorifies what God has done in the past but resists what God is doing in the present. Let us not be like the religious opponents of

Jesus, who put confidence in their natural ability to interpret the Scriptures. It has been said that we have more faith in the devil's ability to deceive us than we have in the Holy Spirit's ability to lead us. We ought to do something about that. May we put our confidence in the power of Christ and in His Spirit to teach us His Word; these should be the present priorities of our lives. May God grant us the grace in this generation to say with the apostle Paul:

> My message and my preaching were not with wise and persuasive words, but with a demonstration of the Spirit's power, so that your faith might not rest on men's wisdom, but on God's power.
> —1 CORINTHIANS 2:4–5

> Jews demand miraculous signs and Greeks look for wisdom, but we preach Christ crucified: a stumbling block to Jews and foolishness to Gentiles, but to those whom God has called, both Jews and Greeks, Christ the power of God and the wisdom of God.
> —1 CORINTHIANS 1:22–24

On the other hand, the Greeks of Paul's day, like modern non-charismatic evangelicals, looked for wisdom in the Word and theology; Paul gave God's answers for both of these streams then, and it is no less relevant today: "But we preach Christ crucified"—Christ, the power of God and the wisdom of God; Word and Spirit. Only in the cross of Christ will we find the true remarriage or union of the Word and the Spirit.

All of them were filled with the Holy Spirit and began to speak in other tongues as the Spirit enabled them.

—Acts 2:4

Then Peter stood up with the Eleven, raised his voice and addressed the crowd: "Fellow Jews and all of you who live in Jerusalem, let me explain this to you; listen carefully to what I say."

—Acts 2:14

Four

THE PREACHING OF THE WORD AND THE SPIRIT

by R. T. Kendall

I HAVE A COUPLE of fears about addressing the subject of the preaching of the Word and the Spirit. The first fear is that I could have fallen prey to the "Peter principle"—having been promoted to the level of my incompetence—in trying to make any contribution with regard to preaching. I want to make clear that I shall be addressing *not how I do it,* but *how it ought to be done.*

My second fear, which is also humbling but puts me in my place, can be seen in these words: "Those who can, do; those who can't, teach." So you may regard this as teaching.

I want to talk about experimental preaching, which

of course I will have to define straight away. No one has improved upon Phillip Brooks' definition of preaching, which he gave in his historic Yale lectures a number of years ago. He defined *preaching* as "the bringing of truth through personality." I would define *experimental preaching* as "releasing the Holy Spirit to be Himself." By *experimental preaching* I do not merely mean experiential preaching. I regard preaching as an experiment, a test of whether or not the Holy Spirit can get past me.

If you look at my congregation at Westminster Chapel, for fifteen years we have only grown a little. I think of other people who can address the subject of preaching—they have really done something. Judge what is written here not on the basis of my experience but by whether it is true. So I want to talk about a kind of preaching that I aspire to.

Now let me explain what I mean by *experimental preaching*. Following Aristotle, experimental preaching assumes a thesis or major premise, then a minor premise, or hypothesis, and then a conclusion. My thesis is that the Holy Spirit wants to be Himself to the people I address. The minor premise is that I am the instrument of the Holy Spirit. The conclusion is that the Spirit becomes Himself to those I address.

CHARISMA OR CHRISMA?

EXPERIMENTAL PREACHING is the same as what our fathers called *unction*. Oddly enough, the word *unction* is used only twice in the New Testament, first in 1 John 2:20 and again in 1 John 2:27. In neither place does the meaning fit with what is generally meant by "unction." Unction comes from the Greek word *chrisma,* which means "anointed." The root word is *chrio,* from which we get the name *Christ*—"anointed one." There are other Greek words like *parrhesia*—"boldness, freedom." Or even various forms of *logos,* which often better express what our fathers called "unction"—thus Paul expressed the wish that he would be given "utterance" *(logos)* in Ephesians 6:19 (KJV).

If we look at the two verses at the start of this chapter, we can see that Acts 2:4 says, "All of them were filled with the Holy Spirit and began to speak in other tongues as the Spirit enabled them." The King James Version says, "...as the Spirit gave them utterance." In the Greek, utterance is a present infinitive that literally means, "to utter." The literal translation reads: "They spoke in other languages as they were enabled to utter." The exact same word appears in Acts 2:14, except that it's not an infinitive. There we read, "Peter stood up...and addressed the crowd." The King James Version simply says, "Peter...standing up...said," but it is the same word as in Acts 2:4.

Now the point is this. What the one hundred twenty could do only as the Spirit enabled them—utter words in other languages—is what Peter did as he preached in his own language on the day of Pentecost. In order for Peter to speak powerfully in his own language, he had to have the same power that enabled the one hundred twenty to speak miraculously in other languages. Peter spoke in his own language—but he possessed the same ability to utter the words.

We are talking about very unusual power, power that I have never experienced, but power that is present when the Spirit is released to be Himself.

However, I would argue that the Greek word *chrisma* is still a valid word for experimental preaching (1 John 2:20, 27). It comes from a root word that refers to the act of smearing as with an ointment. The psalmist referred to the "precious oil poured on the head, running down on Aaron's beard" (Ps. 133:2).

Chrisma is not the same thing as *charismata*. It doesn't even come from the same Greek word. It is not the same thing as *charisma,* which could be a natural thing. It would seem that people are more interested today in the *charismata* or the *charisma* than in this self-effacing quality that is inherent in the anointing for which we long. It is my view that this kind of anointing upon preaching is what is needed most above all else at the present time. Were this dimension to be recovered by the modern pulpit, it would do more to restore public respect for the church and the Christian faith than anything else I know.

In my view, unction alone will open new vistas to make truly great preaching a reality. My thesis then is that the Holy Spirit wants to be Himself and reach those I address unhindered, ungrieved, unquenched, and undisguised. It lies within my power to hinder or release the Spirit. The question is, Will I block the Spirit or let Him get past me?

There's a famous story that will illustrate what I mean. John Calvin wrote a letter to Martin Luther. He had not met him, but he regarded him as his father in the gospel. Calvin made some suggestions to Luther on the doctrine of the Lord's Supper. I wish that Luther had received Calvin's letter—Luther needed what Calvin had to say about it. But it has been said that Philip Melancthon, who was at Luther's side, rightly or wrongly intercepted it, read it, and never let Luther see it, regarding it as too sensitive for the aging Luther to read.

Now we too can do that sort of thing with those we address. We may be afraid to let our hearers experience what the Spirit would be and do. We may block the Spirit from being Himself.

Vince Lombardi, who was the greatest coach American football history has ever seen, was asked his secret to winning so many football games. He replied, "Winning is not the main thing; it is the only thing." I would put to you that this is the need of the hour with regard to preaching. We must desire this element, this dimension, this anointing; it should be what we want more than anything and what we aspire to more than any goal that we could conceive.

Said the apostle Paul:

> My message and my preaching were not with wise and persuasive words, but with a demonstration of the Spirit's power.
>
> —1 CORINTHIANS 2:4

> Our gospel came to you not simply with words, but also with power, with the Holy Spirit and with deep conviction.
>
> —1 THESSALONIANS 1:5

Paul also said, and this bothers me, that he wanted to preach "not with words of human wisdom, lest the cross of Christ be emptied of its power" (1 Cor. 1:17).

Would I not be right in saying that this kind of preaching is something exceedingly rare today? For all I know, it is something that cannot be transmitted by the printed page or through tape recordings. If you were to read a sermon by George Whitefield and didn't know it was he who wrote it, you would not go across the street to hear him preach. I never will forget the first time I looked at Whitefield's sermons; I read one page and found very little substance, and thought, *Oh, well, it's Whitefield, I'll try another page.* I kept reading, finished the sermon, and thought, *What on earth is this?* I read the other sermons, and I couldn't believe it. The same is undoubtedly true of John Sung, the man who saw a great revival in China forty years ago. I met a man who was converted under John Sung, and he would talk to me about him, describing his sermons and their impact. I longed for the day when I could read some of John Sung's sermons. Finally I got a copy; they seemed utterly devoid of substantial content.

Some years ago I heard a story of an American couple who crossed the Atlantic some two hundred years ago, hoping to hear George Whitefield preach in his own church, his Tabernacle in Tottenham Court Road. The couple said they had a very rough crossing. They came into Southampton very tired, but they inquired whether George Whitefield would be in his pulpit on Sunday. The word came that he would be there, so they arrived at the Tabernacle the next day, still tired from their journey, and sat and listened to George Whitefield. They said that when he stood up he also appeared tired. They thought perhaps he'd been very busy and hadn't had time to prepare. At first his sermon seemed very rambling, and they thought, *What have we done, coming here?* But at some point during the sermon something happened. It was indescribable. The atmosphere was heavenly. They said they would have crossed a thousand seas to be there. They left the Tabernacle physically refreshed from the journey. It is reported that someone went up to Mr. Whitefield and asked for permission to print his sermon. Whitefield replied, "Yes, if you can get in the thunder and the lightning."

Dr. Martyn Lloyd-Jones called this unction an "access of power." It is God acting. I remind you of my thesis: The Holy Spirit wants to be Himself to the people I address. "The spirit is willing, but the body is weak" (Matt. 26:41). And yet I am the instrument of the Spirit; I stand between God and men either to intercept or to transmit what the Spirit wants to be and to do. If I do not block the Spirit, He will be Himself to my hearers.

HOW DO I BLOCK THE SPIRIT?

I BELIEVE THERE are seven ways that the Spirit can be blocked in our preaching. I am the world's expert on this!

1. HUMAN WISDOM

First, the Spirit can be blocked by "words of human wisdom." Speaking personally, this is one of my greatest temptations, especially when nearly all I utter publicly is tape recorded and will likely be in print. So the temptation for me is to write a book rather than preach a sermon. This encourages a lop-sided emphasis on the correct use of words.

The apostle Paul was one of the greatest intellectuals

in the history of the world, one of the greatest rhetoricians of all time. If anybody had the ability to speak with the "wisdom of words," it was he. Read 1 Corinthians 13. But if Paul made any effort at all, it was in being careful not to speak in such a manner that would call attention to the well-turned phrase rather than call attention to the cross. The great Charles Spurgeon used to say, "Labor to be plain."

There are three rules here: Don't try to be eloquent. Don't try to be eloquent. Don't try to be eloquent!

2. PERVERTING THE TEXT

We block the Spirit if we don't allow the true meaning of the text to flow unhindered. The anointed preacher should be like a clear window pane that calls no attention to itself, but it enables others to see right through it. When we distort the text, we're like cracked windows or, worse, stained-glass windows that are never intended to be seen through.

We can mishandle a text three ways. First, by treating a verse contrary to its context. Second, by importing an idea, however valid, that the text did not call for. Third, by superimposing our own idea upon the text.

The text was written by the Spirit, and the Spirit knows what it means. It is my duty to find out the meaning of the text, not to sound clever or to import an idea or superimpose my idea onto the text. The text must speak for itself.

3. COPYING OTHERS

I block the Holy Spirit when I am not myself or

when I try to imitate someone else. We tend so often to suppose that there is a quality in another that we think is not in ourselves. We see it in another person and pick up his mannerisms and think, *I'm going to be like that and everyone's going to think I'm like him.*

There was a preacher in Texas who was powerful. He had an anointing on him. But when he got going and preached with such power—nobody knew why he did this—his left hand would come up over his ear. He'd just keep on preaching. They made that man professor of preaching at Southwestern Baptist Theological Seminary in Fort Worth, Texas. And you could always tell one of his students. When those young men thought they were "ringing the bell," that left hand would go up over the ear!

I told that story at Southwestern Baptist Theological Seminary, hoping to pull the story out of the woodwork. And it worked. An old professor came up to me right after the service. He said, "I know exactly who you mean."

I said, "Well, would you please tell me why that left hand would go over his left ear?"

He said, "It's very simple. He was hard of hearing, and he could hear himself better when he spoke like that."

But those young men didn't know that. They were simply imitating a weird habit.

Dr. Lloyd-Jones told a similar story. He said, "Back in the twenties, there was a man in South Wales who had an eccentric habit. When he used to preach, hair would get down in his eyes. He wouldn't take his hand and push it back, he would just shake it back. And sure enough, there were young preachers all over South Wales who, when they were preaching, would shake their head." Lloyd-Jones said that one student actually was bald, but he too shook his head!

It is the hardest thing in the world for me to come to terms with my own personality; it is very humbling for me to admit that I am not Martyn Lloyd-Jones, to accept myself, and risk what people will think if I am myself. And yet I have come to see that I block the Spirit when I am not myself. God made me the way I am; He made you the way you are—He threw the mold away when He made you. We need to learn this. We dignify Him when we accept ourselves. When you learn to like yourself, God likes that. He looks down and says, "Well, I'm glad you like yourself—you know, I made you that way." And so we affirm Him.

4. AVOIDING DIFFICULT SCRIPTURES

We block the Holy Spirit by not following through with the obvious meaning of the text and its implications. I suspect that some preachers don't like to preach through a book in the Bible or through a chapter verse by verse because they're afraid to face up to a verse that they know will be coming up. They may not know what the verse means, or they may be afraid to discuss what it means. And so they jump around the Scriptures instead. Sometimes it takes courage to pass on the plain meaning of the text to the hearers. We may think that it will rob us of a chance to be eloquent, but to do otherwise will rob them of the simple truth that all our hearers have a right to hear.

We want to master a text, but *great preachers are mastered by the text*. When we are mastered by the text, we will state plainly what the text is saying and follow through with the application that the Holy Spirit dictates, even if that preaching gets close to the bone and threatens our own lifestyle. Often we will not preach on a subject because we know there is something in our lives that will be obvious, and we dare not preach on it. I am convinced that a lot of preachers will not preach on tithing because they are not tithers. There are a lot of preachers who will not preach on witnessing because they don't do it. And so it is, when it comes to certain verses, we don't like to preach that which will expose our hearts. That is why the Spirit doesn't get through us.

The Reformers accused Rome of keeping the Bible from the common people, but we do the same thing if we don't pass on the obvious meaning of the text.

5. PERSONAL FEELINGS

I block the Spirit when I let a personal concern or emotional involvement get in the way of my preaching. This is sometimes called preaching *at* the people, which will never do.

There are five options available to the preacher:

1. Preaching *for* the people. That's *performance.*
2. Preaching *at* the people. That's *lack of self-control.*
3. Preaching *down to* the people. That's *arrogance.*
4. Preaching *up to* the people. That's *fear.*
5. But there is a transaction that takes place between the throne of grace and the pew

when we preach *to* the people. That is *our calling*.

Preaching *at* the people blocks the Spirit and leaves the people oppressed; it is always counterproductive. I know because I've done it. The temptation is to put the record straight. It is a melancholy enterprise called "self-vindication." It is assuming that the pulpit is my own platform. James Stewart, in his book *Preaching,* quotes Bernard Manning: "The pulpit is no more the minister's than the communion table is his."

I block the Spirit when I do not allow the ungrieved Spirit to master my mind in preparation, controlling my own feelings in the act of preaching.

6. GRIEVING THE SPIRIT

That brings us to the sixth way we can block the Spirit. I block the Spirit when I do not let the Spirit master my mind in preparation. The Holy Spirit is obviously a very sensitive Person—in fact the most sensitive Person that ever was.

We often say of a sensitive person, "You'd better watch what you say around him." We see sensitivity as a defect in another person, calling that person hypersensitive. But the Holy Spirit is a bit like that. It is alarming that we almost never know, at the time, that we are grieving the Spirit. We don't feel a thing. When Samson gave his secret to Delilah, he didn't feel a thing: "He did not know that the LORD had left him" (Judg. 16:20).

The chief way we grieve the Spirit is by bitterness and holding a grudge. A number of years ago I went through what was, at the time, the greatest trial I've ever known. I was in a situation where someone had done something that wasn't very nice. I couldn't talk about it to anybody. But an old friend from Romania came through London, and because he was from outside London I thought, *Well, I'll tell Josif.*

I have to tell you, the only reason I told it to Josif was so that he would pat me on the shoulder and say, "R. T., that's right. Good. Get it out. Go on, just let it out—I'd be angry, too." And so I told him what you will never know.

He pointed a finger and said, "R. T., you must totally forgive them. For until you totally forgive them, you will be in chains. Release them, and you will be released."

Nobody had ever talked to me like that in my life. But I knew I could trust Josif's analysis of the situation. "Wounds from a friend can be trusted" (Prov. 27:6).

And then I said, "Josif, I can't. Oh, Josif, there's something else I forgot to tell you. Let me..."

He interrupted me, saying, "R. T., you must totally forgive them."

It was the hardest thing I ever had to do. It didn't happen in one hour. But I did it. And when it happened, do you know that the way the Spirit flooded my soul brought me back to the way I had felt years ago.

Peter said, "Husbands, in the same way be considerate as you live with your wives...so that nothing will hinder your prayers" (1 Pet. 3:7). I know what it's like to have a quarrel with my wife. Once when we got into an argument, I slammed the door, went to my office, got out my pen and said, "Holy Spirit, now help me to write this sermon I've got to preach tomorrow." I just sat there. It was awful. After about forty-five minutes I went back into the living room and I said, "I'm sorry."

When I went back into my den to pray, the thoughts were coming quicker than I could write them down.

I block the Spirit when I do not let the Spirit master my mind in preparation. When I'm angry, when I'm holding a grudge, when I have not totally forgiven the person who has hurt me deeply, then I have grieved the Spirit.

Bitterness always seems right at the time. When we say something about another person that reduces their credibility we don't feel a thing. But later when we try to do something we thought we were able to do, we find it's being done in our own strength—like Samson—and it's useless.

Sometimes I define spirituality as "closing the time gap between sin and repentance." In other words, how long does it take you to admit you were wrong? For some it takes years, for some seconds, and for most of us it's somewhere in between. Often, when you know something about the way the Spirit can be grieved, you can catch yourself and narrow the time gap to seconds, so that there's no discontinuity with the ungrieved Spirit resident in you.

When the Spirit is Himself in me, it is because He is ungrieved and therefore can master my mind in preparation. When this is the case my preparation is sheer delight; thoughts come—original insights I could never have thought of—because the Holy Spirit wrote the Bible, and He knows what it means.

7. TRYING TO KEEP THE CONTROL

Finally, I block the Spirit when I do not let Him master me in my delivery. This means to have the courage to pass on what the ungrieved Spirit gave me in preparation. It means the refusal to let any personal concerns come between me and my congregation when I preach. It can also mean the willingness to depart from my prepared notes and, if necessary, ruin my sermon.

Like the ointment on Aaron's beard, it may be sticky and alter my appearance or injure my pride. Do you have any idea what the robe of the high priest looked like? It was ornate; it was beautiful. Psalm 133 talks about the ointment poured on Aaron's head, flowing down on Aaron's beard and upon his robe, soiling it. I am not prepared to do that to one of my sermons! But this dimension is what can, in the end, test the experiment, test whether the Spirit can be Himself to those I address.

In my view, experimental preaching will include all three of the elements to which Aristotle refers in his work *Rhetoric: ethos, pathos, logos.*

- *Ethos*—refers to the credibility of the speaker
- *Pathos*—the appeal to the senses, as long as this is done with integrity
- *Logos*—the reason or logic of the message

Some sermons today are devoid of *logos* and long on *pathos.* And some are strong on *logos*—correctness of doctrine—but without any *pathos.*

When the Holy Spirit is released to be Himself, we will not only have the needed balance but the satisfaction that those we address will hear a word from beyond, which defies a natural explanation.

God also said to Abraham, "As for Sarai your wife, you are no longer to call her Sarai; her name will be Sarah. I will bless her and will surely give you a son by her. I will bless her so that she will be the mother of nations; kings of peoples will come from her." Abraham fell facedown; he laughed and said to himself, "Will a son be born to a man a hundred years old? Will Sarah bear a child at the age of ninety?" And Abraham said to God, "If only Ishmael might live under your blessing!"

—GENESIS 17:15–18

Five

A Post-Charismatic Era

by R. T. Kendall

NEVER IN MY life had I known fear and trembling as I felt in the days before I originally gave this message. Peace to move on in my preparation came only as I allowed the Holy Spirit to point me to Genesis 17:18. It is the only theme that gripped me. I knew that I had to speak on it. My message in this chapter is a statement—not a sermon—a statement that I believe to be prophetic. I was not given to talking like that, nor am I yet, but I knew that what I had to say was true and would come to pass.

I am forecasting a new era, one that can be called a *post-charismatic era.*

When I use the term *charismatic,* I want it to be shorthand for the work of the Spirit that we've all known about throughout this century. It was originally called "the Pentecostal movement." In the sixties, certainly in America, it was called "the Glossolalia movement," from the Greek word *glossa,* meaning "tongue." In more recent years, it has been known as "the Charismatic movement."

I once had a meal with a well-known charismatic leader. Quite spontaneously I put this question to him: "If the Charismatic movement is Ishmael or Isaac, which do you think it is?"

He answered, "Isaac."

I said to him, "What if I told you that the Charismatic movement is not Isaac but Ishmael?"

His answer was, "I hope not."

I said to him, "You convince me more than ever that the Charismatic movement *is* Ishmael."

This man, a Spirit-filled, godly man, responded exactly as Abraham did: "And Abraham said to God, 'If only Ishmael might live under your blessing!'" (Gen. 17:18).

What Abraham had wanted more than anything in the world was being handed to him on a silver platter: the promise of a son through his beloved wife, Sarah. And he was now rejecting it! When God's promise was originally given, I'm sure Abraham would never have believed that one day he would react so negatively to something so positive.

> God also said to Abraham, "As for Sarai your wife, you are no longer to call her Sarai; her name will be Sarah. I will bless her and will surely give you a son by her. I will bless her so

that she will be the mother of nations; kings of peoples will come from her." Abraham fell face-down; he laughed and said to himself, "Will a son be born to a man a hundred years old? Will Sarah bear a child at the age of ninety?" And Abraham said to God, "If only Ishmael might live under your blessing!"

—GENESIS 17:15–18

ABRAHAM BELIEVED GOD'S WORD

FOR THIRTEEN YEARS Abraham sincerely believed that Ishmael was the promised son. It all began about twenty-five years earlier when he was given a promise; believing that promise meant that righteousness was put to his credit.

After this, the word of the LORD came to Abram in a vision: "Do not be afraid, Abram. I am your shield, your very great reward." But Abram said, "O Sovereign LORD, what can you give me since I remain childless and the one who will inherit my estate is Eliezer of Damascus?" And Abram said, "You have given me no children; so a servant in my household will be my heir." Then the word of the LORD came to him: "This man will not be your heir, but a son coming from your own body will be your heir." He took him outside and said, "Look up at the heavens, and count the stars—if indeed you can count them." Then he said to him, "So shall your offspring be." Abram believed the LORD, and he credited it to him as righteousness.

—GENESIS 15:1–6

By believing the promise, righteousness was put to Abraham's credit. That became the apostle Paul's chief illustration for the doctrine of justification by faith. It was what Martin Luther rediscovered in the sixteenth century, and the world was turned upside down. By believing that Jesus died on the cross for our sins, and transferring all the hope that we once had placed in our works onto what Jesus did for us on the cross, by putting all of our eggs into one basket—"Jesus died for me"—by believing that, righteousness is put to our credit as though we had never sinned. And that is the gospel.

Abraham really believed that promise. But the years were rolling by. No son. Sarah was getting older. No son. She reached the age past which it was not normally possible for a woman to bear a child. Abraham and Sarah were both discouraged. We all get discouraged when God delays fulfillment of His word. We all tend to fret during the era of unanswered prayer. We all know the pain of waiting, having been sure that we have got it right. Abraham was so sure when God said, "I will surely bless you and make your descendants as numerous as the stars in the sky and as the sand on the seashore" (Gen. 22:17). But nothing was happening.

One day Sarah came up with a solution.

> Now Sarai, Abram's wife, had borne him no children. But she had an Egyptian maidservant named Hagar; so she said to Abram, "The LORD has kept me from having children. Go, sleep with my maidservant; perhaps I can build a family through her." Abram agreed to what Sarai said. So after Abram had been living in

Canaan ten years, Sarai his wife took her Egyptian maidservant Hagar and gave her to her husband to be his wife. He slept with Hagar, and she conceived.

—GENESIS 16:1–4

Abraham did not initiate this idea; it was entirely Sarah's. Why did he agree to it? Because he really did believe the promise that was given to him, and he became willing to see it happen any way God chose to bring it about. And what is more, if Hagar's child happened to be a male, it would have come from Abraham's own body, and that was the promise. There was every reason to believe that God was at work. A male child would fit the promise of Genesis 15:4–5.

Hagar conceived, but Sarah had second thoughts:

[Abram] slept with Hagar, and she conceived. When she knew she was pregnant, she began to despise her mistress. Then Sarai said to Abram, "You are responsible for the wrong I am suffering. I put my servant in your arms, and now that she knows she is pregnant, she despises me. May the LORD judge between you and me."

—GENESIS 16:4–5

Hagar despised Sarah; Sarah persecuted Hagar. Hagar fled to the desert. An angel of the Lord visited her. He then announced to Hagar, "You are now with child...You shall name him Ishmael, for the LORD has heard of your misery" (Gen. 16:11).

Four things can be said at this stage:

- Sarah persecuted Hagar.
- God affirmed Hagar.
- The child was male.
- The seal of God was on Ishmael. Abraham could never forget this.

Ishmael was born when Abraham was eighty-six years old. As far as Abraham was concerned, God had kept His word. There could be no doubt about it. Everything pointed to Ishmael's being the promised son. And so Abraham said to God, "If only Ishmael might live under your blessing."

Abraham was not only reconciled to the suggestion that Hagar should be the mother of his son, but he saw that it met every condition of the promise of Genesis 15:4—every condition he ever imagined. Genesis 15:4, as far as Abraham was concerned, was now ancient history—it was done. God had kept His word—that was that. Ishmael met the requirements, and Abraham had no complaints.

One day Abraham got up like on any other morning, unprepared for what would happen on that day. What a difference a day makes! He was now ninety-nine years old. Ishmael was a teenager. He was Abraham's pride and joy. Never underestimate how much Abraham loved Ishmael, his one and only son. But out of the blue, God appeared to him.

When Abram was ninety-nine years old, the LORD appeared to him and said, "I am God Almighty; walk before me and be blameless. I will confirm my covenant between me and you and will greatly increase your numbers." Abram fell facedown, and God said to him, "As for me, this is my covenant with you: You will be the father of many nations. No longer will you be called Abram; your name will be Abraham."

—GENESIS 17:1–5

So Abraham enjoyed every word that he heard on that day. God gave him the covenant of circumcision, the wonderful promise that he would be the father of many nations; the land of Canaan would be an everlasting possession; he loved every moment of it. Everything was going fine with Abraham.

No problem about the circumcision—he would circumcise Ishmael, and he himself would be circumcised; the covenant would extend to his household, even to foreigners who became a part of his household.

The covenant was inflexible—not to keep it was to be cut off—fine. So far, so good.

But then came some news for which Abraham was totally unprepared. It ought to have been the grandest, most sublime, most fantastic promise that his ears would ever hear. But he couldn't believe what he was hearing, and he didn't like it. God said to Abraham:

> "As for Sarai your wife, you are no longer to call her Sarai, her name will be Sarah. I will bless her and will surely give you a son by her…" Abraham fell facedown; he laughed and said to himself, "Will a son be born to a man a hundred years old? Will Sarah bear a child at the age of ninety?…If only Ishmael might live under your blessing!"
>
> —GENESIS 17:15–18

69

Abraham's little world was now turned upside down. He was uttering an impassioned, painful plea, "Please let the covenant be fulfilled in Ishmael."

I am prepared to say now that this is precisely what God is saying to us at the present time. Sarah, whom the apostle Paul called "the mother of us all," will conceive. However much we love Ishmael, however much God affirmed Ishmael, and however much Ishmael fits the promise, God is up to something new—God is in Ishmael, but Ishmael is not God's ultimate purpose. Sarah will conceive. Isaac is on the way.

THE CHARISMATIC ERA

LET'S RETURN TO my friend who hoped that the Charismatic movement was Isaac. I said to him, "Why should this make you so sad? When we consider what God is up to next, that it will be far greater—as Isaac was to Ishmael—what will it be like when God does something in the land unprecedented, not even thought about? If Ishmael could give Abraham so much joy, how much more Isaac? If Ishmael had been blessed by God, how much more Isaac?"

And so today when we consider how God has blessed the church through the Charismatic and Pentecostal movements, and how many wonderful and thrilling things have come during this era, what will Isaac be like?

WHY SHOULD THE CHARISMATIC ERA BE AFFIRMED?

FIRST, ABRAHAM did not initiate the era of Ishmael. Abraham was an honorable man. Abraham did believe God's promise. And we should honor Sarah, the mother of us all, who was the instigator of the whole thing. The promise of a son came to Abraham as a word from God. Furthermore, God's affirmation of Ishmael to Hagar proves it was of God.

The charismatic era is what God did. We're all the better for it. Most churches worth their salt today in England are largely charismatic. The greatest hymnody this century has seen has emerged from the charismatic movement. When you consider that the widespread revival, particularly in the Third World— Africa, Latin America, South America, Indonesia, and Korea—is largely pentecostal, you can see why we should affirm the charismatic era.

Second, Sarah persecuted Hagar. Have you any idea just how much Charismatics and Pentecostals have suffered? Pentecostals, neo-Pentecostals, those who dare talk about the gifts of the Spirit, signs, wonders, and miracles, have been outside the camp, like Hagar in the desert. They have been put down, lied about, misunderstood, persecuted as much as those in any era in the history of the Christian church.

Third, Hagar was affirmed by an undoubted divine visitation in the desert. She could look up to God through her tears. I love the way the King James Version puts it; it moves me almost to tears every time I read it: Hagar "called the name of the LORD that spake unto her, Thou God seest me" (Gen. 16:13, KJV).

Hagar knew that God had given her a son. God even gave the son the name "God hears." God left Hagar in no doubt that He was with her, that He was behind it all. And those who unashamedly regard themselves as charismatic know that God has visited

71

them; God has affirmed them. They have seen the supernatural. My heart warms to them; they are among my closest friends. Don't tell me it is all worked up; don't tell me there are no signs and wonders—that is not so.

Fourth, God had a secret purpose for Ishmael that was revealed first to Hagar and later to Abraham.

> As for Ishmael, I have heard you: I will surely bless him; I will make him fruitful and will greatly increase his numbers. He will be the father of twelve rulers, and I will make him into a great nation. But my covenant I will establish with Isaac.
>
> —GENESIS 17:20–21

And God said to Hagar, in Genesis 16:10, "I will so increase your descendants that they will be too numerous to count." And by the way, we haven't seen the end of this yet. The natural, literal, Arabic descendants of Ishmael are too numerous to count. They have spread in ever-increasing numbers, their mosques and places of worship are going up in rapid fashion in every major city. Who knows what the end will be? We are going to see Islam turning to Christ before it is all over. "No eye has seen, no ear has heard, no mind has conceived what God has prepared for those who love him—but God has revealed it to us by his Spirit" (1 Cor. 2:9–10).

THE POST-CHARISMATIC ERA

NOW I WANT to show you why Ishmael was not meant to be the promised child.

First, God wanted the promise of the gospel as revealed to Abraham to be fulfilled in a manner that defied a natural explanation. Conversion is the greatest miracle that can happen under the sun. It is a sovereign work of God; it is what God does. When Hagar conceived it was natural, but when Sarah conceived it defied a natural explanation; only God could have done it.

Second, God wanted the heirs of the gospel to look back on what He did in a manner no one would question. Understandable though it was for Abraham to agree with Sarah's proposal, there would always be a cloud over it. Even Abraham must have questioned, "Was this really the right thing to do? Is this all there is? Is this really what God had in mind when He gave the promise in Genesis 15:5?" I don't mean to be unfair, but though the presence of the supernatural is not to be denied, one must admit that the real, undoubted, empirical proof of signs and wonders is not all that common.

Third, what is often overlooked is what the promise of Isaac eventually did for Abraham—it drove him back to God's Word. In Romans chapter 4, the apostle Paul, having dealt with Genesis 15:6 to show the basis of his doctrine of justification by faith, suddenly jumps to the time when Abraham was reconciled to the fact that Isaac was on the way.

> Against all hope, Abraham in hope believed and so became the father of many nations, just as it had been said to him, "So shall your offspring be." Without weakening in his faith, he faced the fact that his body was as good as dead—since he was about a hundred years

> old—and that Sarah's womb was also dead. Yet
> he did not waver through unbelief regarding
> the promise of God, but was strengthened in
> his faith and gave glory to God, being fully per-
> suaded that God had power to do what he had
> promised. This is why "it was credited to him
> as righteousness."
>
> —ROMANS 4:18–22

It was credited to him as righteousness when he believed the first time. But now he is believing *again,* and he goes back to God's original promise. Abraham now has something to live for that exceeds his greatest expectation. For over the years, Abraham had underestimated the word—the dignity of it, the glory of it. But with the promise of Isaac on the way, once he became reconciled to what God said was going to happen next, it drove him back to the Word.

I predict that if we will accept this word, many will get back to the Word of God as they have not done for years. They will have a new romance with the Scriptures. It will be like falling in love all over again. It will result in a fresh assurance, a burst of power, expectancy that you never dreamed possible. And we will have something to live for unlike anything we have ever known.

Fourth, the post-charismatic era will be charac- terised by an awe with regard to the Word that is equal to the awe we think we now have towards the supernatural. When the Word and the Spirit coalesce, it will be a remarriage of what should never have been separated. As with human marriage, God said "What God has joined together, let man not sepa- rate" (Matt. 19:6). What then will the post-charismatic era be like? It will be an era in which the Word preached will be more awesome than the vindication of God's name. It will be an era in which signs and wonders will not be under a cloud of suspicion but open to the minutest scrutiny. As the New Testament skeptics said of the miracle of the crippled man who suddenly was walking, "We cannot deny it" (Acts 4:16).

It will be an era when the gospel, not signs and wonders, will be the front runner of priorities among God's ministers. It will be an era when conversion to Christ will not be minimized, but seen as the greatest miracle that can happen. It will be an era in which the most difficult cases imaginable will be turned into putty in the hands of a sovereign God; when surprising conversions become common. It will be an era when the world will fear the prayers of God's people more than they fear nuclear war. It was said that Mary, Queen of Scots, feared John Knox's prayers more than an army of ten thousand men.

The post-charismatic era will be a time when government and people in high places will come on bended knee to God's people and ask for help. With Ishmael it was the promise of a nation; with Isaac it was the promise of many nations. The apostle Paul said that Isaac is the "heir of the world" (Rom. 4:13). We're talking about something big. We're talking about something that is wider than one nation's boundaries, when kings of the earth, leaders of nations, are made to see that there is a God in the heavens. It will be an era in which children will be sovereign vessels. An era when ordinary Christians are equipped with prophetic gifts. It won't be a case of superstars vying for TV time, trying to be seen or heard, or trying to prove themselves. We're talking about an awakening that reaches areas, people, and places, which heretofore were impenetrable, without the aid of the media and public relations men or the endorsement of high-profile people.

The post-charismatic era will be an era in which the glory of the Lord covers the earth as the waters cover the sea.

> The LORD replied: "Write down the revelation...so that a herald may run with it. For the revelation awaits an appointed time; it speaks of the end and will not prove false. Though it linger, wait for it; it will certainly come and will not delay."
>
> —HABAKKUK 2:2–3

"O that Ishmael might live under your blessing!" God said, "Isaac will be the one." The name *Isaac* means "he laughs." I do not believe it will be long before it can be said openly, "We have a pregnancy," when cynical laughter will turn to reverent fear and joy.

I will worship toward thy holy temple, and praise thy name for thy lovingkindness and for thy truth: for thou hast magnified thy word above all thy name.

—PSALM 138:2, KJV

Six

THE WORD AND THE NAME

by Paul Cain

I F THE DAY of Pentecost was all that great, then
what on earth will the last-day ministry be like?
Pentecost was only a partial fulfillment of the
prophecy that sons and daughters would prophesy,
young men would see visions, old men would dream
dreams, and the Lord would pour His Spirit out
upon all (Joel 2:28).

I am nervous about missing anything that God
has. The Charismatic movement has been great. It has
crossed all denominational lines, and through it God
has brought so many people into deeper dimensions
of His power and His love. But if there is something
greater, then we should be very happy about it.

"Therefore since the promise of entering his rest still stands, let us be careful that none of you be found to have fallen short of it" (Heb. 4:1). The inspired psalmist is recording a neglected truth too staggering for even some of the translators of the Bible, such as the translators of the New International Version, for instance. Only the King James Version and the Living Bible rendered it accurately—"thou hast magnified thy word above all thy name." I wonder if we really believe that the psalmist meant exactly what he said, what is actually recorded in Psalm 138:2? Dr. Kendall and other Bible scholars, those who know the Hebrew best, have informed me that the King James Version got it right. What on earth could be greater than the name of Jesus? What could be greater than God's name? But here we learn that God magnifies— exalts—His Word above all His name.

There is a difference between God's Word and God's name. Have you ever thought about this difference, or even about the difference between your word and your name? God's Word has to do with His integrity, His honor, His honesty—that is to say, His character. It is impossible for God to lie. Jesus could say, "Verily, verily I say unto you...." He is the only preacher who ever lived who could say "Amen, amen," before He ever said anything, because He knew that everything He was going to say was absolutely true.

On the other hand, the name of God refers mainly to His influence, His reputation, His power. "You may ask me for anything in my name, and I will do it" (John 14:14). In Acts 3:16 a man is miraculously healed in Jesus' name: "It is Jesus' name and the faith that comes through him that has given this complete healing to him, as you can all see."

My mother, who lived to be one hundred five, taught me a lot of wonderful things. One of the things she taught me was Proverbs 22:1: "A good name is more desirable than great riches." Remember, the name of God has to do with His power, with His reputation in this world. Remember that the Word of God has to do with His integrity, His honesty, and His character.

God cares about both His Word and His name, His Word and His Spirit. God cares about His integrity and His influence, but compared side by side, I assure you that God's integrity is more important to Him than His reputation. How do we know this? God often allows His reputation to suffer for years and years without vindicating Himself. And we all know that He has the power at any given moment to call legions of angels to cause "things which are not" to appear, and to do miraculous feats that only He can do. He is a God of miracles, a God of power. And at any given moment He could cause a revival situation similar to the days of Ananias and Sapphira in the first part of Acts, where a man and his wife lied to the Holy Spirit and both fell dead. There was great fear in those days: "Great fear seized the whole church and all who heard about these events" (Acts 5:11). So we see that God is being merciful to the church in her present state, to withhold the vindication of His name even to the point of letting men drag His name through the mud.

How many have said, "If God is just, why did He allow this to happen?" or "Why did my baby die?" or "Why did my wife die of cancer?" or "Why did my husband die of this deadly malady?" They say that

81

God has a lot to answer for. "If He's a God of love, why did this happen?" Perhaps you yourself have said, "If there's a God, He has a lot to answer for as far as I'm concerned."

I really enjoyed a situation some time ago when a man said, "I do not believe in the God whom you are preaching about. If there is such a God I have a lot of things I'd like to ask Him."

I said, "Well, just what would you like to ask Him?"

"Well," he said, "I'd like to tell Him a thing or two."

The Spirit of God came, and I said, "You know, I think He would like to tell you a thing or two."

And God told him a thing or two, and the man said, "That's enough."

I said, "Well, what kind of questions would you like to ask Him? He's in this room right now."

He said, "Never mind. Just forget it."

God's reputation, in the eyes of many, leaves much to be desired, so His name actually suffers. God doesn't like His name to suffer, but He's willing to wait for His name to be cleared. God does not suffer from insecurity but is willing to wait for us to find out the truth. Jesus prayed, "Sanctify them by the truth; your word is truth" (John 17:17). It is because the truth is more important to God than His reputation that He magnifies His Word above all of His name.

But the good news is complementary to what R. T. wrote in the last chapter: God is about to clear His name. He is about to do something in the name of the holy child, Jesus. This is called "last-day ministry."

Then will the eyes of the blind be opened and

the ears of the deaf unstopped. Then will the lame leap like a deer, and the mute tongue shout for joy.

—ISAIAH 35:5–6

God will vindicate His name in the name of Jesus. How do we know but what in the days to come we will see hospitals once filled with the crippled bodies of children emptied as those children are instantly made straight in the name of Jesus, made strong just as in the Book of Acts?

What should really matter to us is whether or not we have the honor of God regardless of what men say or think. Jesus said, "How can you believe if you accept praise from one another, yet make no effort to obtain the praise that comes from the only God?" (John 5:44). Do you think that at the judgment seat of Christ, the Lord Jesus is going to stop everything and say, "Oh, well, there's Paul Cain—Paul, you have a wonderful reputation. I'm just so glad you're here. I'm so glad to meet you!" Ridiculous! Not at all! "For by your words you will be acquitted, and by your words you will be condemned" (Matt. 12:37).

There is a judge for the one who rejects me and does not accept my words; that very word which I spoke will condemn him at the last day.

—JOHN 12:48

God knows the truth about us—that's the measuring rod by which we will be judged at the judgment seat of Christ. Have you ever noticed that we tend to judge others by their words and their works, whereas we normally judge ourselves by our intentions? You and I will not be judged on the basis of our reputations.

God has been very interested in His integrity, but in the last days He says, "It will come to pass that I will pour out My Spirit on all people." We have had a significant outpouring of His Holy Spirit during the days of the Pentecostal movement and during the days of the Charismatic movement, for which I am very grateful. God is using pentecostal and charismatic people to reach every stratum of society, and before this thing is over God will see to it that all flesh will be graced by the glorious, exhaustive outpouring upon all flesh. And I say, "Even so, come, Lord Jesus; magnify Your name now."

God spoke to me recently and said, "I am about to clear My name." We are on the brink of an era not unlike that described in 1 Samuel 3:11:

> And the LORD said to Samuel: "See, I am about to do something in Israel that will make the ears of everyone who hears of it tingle."

As Jesus said, "He who has ears to hear, let him hear." All those who hear it, their ears will tingle.

Revelation 6:15–16 describes what will happen when God vindicates His name by His power.

> Then the kings of the earth, the princes, the generals, the rich, the mighty, and every slave and every free man hid in caves and among the rocks of the mountains. They called to the mountains and the rocks, "Fall on us and hide us from the face of him who sits on the throne and from the wrath of the Lamb!"

One day soon every knee shall bow and every tongue confess that Jesus is Lord. Muslims by the millions will soon kneel and say, "Jesus is Lord; Jesus is Lord."

There will be a great number of evangelicals who have been far removed from the pentecostal element and from signs and wonders, all of that has been repugnant to them, but they are going to see the fire of the Lord fall and will say, "The Lord, He is God; we missed out on the first shot but we won't miss out on this!"

There are reputable men in the ministry today who for one reason or another rejected the first voice of God that came to the Charismatics; this time these good men will hear the Lord speaking a second time and will come around and be a part of this glorious era when God clears His name, when Jesus' name is the most powerful, operative, glorious, manifest power in the earth. He will accomplish this through a people who have a greater respect for His Word than they have had for the works of His hands.

I believe that God is going to vindicate His name through the church as we begin to embrace this message in a living way. God is speaking to us, saying the same thing He said to Martha in John 11:40—"Did I not tell you that if you believed, you would see the glory of God?"

"'The glory of this present house will be greater than the glory of the former house,' says the LORD Almighty. 'And in this place I will grant peace'" (Hag. 2:9). Think about the anointing and the unity and the peace that will come when God vindicates His name among His people.

I am doing my best to encourage Charismatics to

live long enough for the post-charismatic era, so that we can see the Lord clear His name. Then it is going to be easy to see all of these wonderful people who are not Charismatics have their questions answered. I tell you we shall see those question marks yanked into exclamation marks when the Lord shows Himself and does His wonderful work in the land.

Why do you think there were no eyewitnesses to the physical resurrection of Jesus? Why do you think God did not allow on-the-spot eyewitnesses to the most important event in the universe? I believe that God did not want the glory of His power to compete with the integrity of His Word. The disciples had no edge on this, but they had to believe just as we have to believe in the resurrection of Jesus Christ. We all have to believe the integrity of His Word to get where we are now. Aren't you glad that you're saved by hearing the gospel and by believing that God raised Jesus from the dead? It is a privilege to be able to believe and see the greatest miracle of all miracles—the salvation of the soul. As Jesus said to Thomas after the resurrection, "Blessed are those who have not seen and yet have believed" (John 20:29).

The miraculous power seems more awesome, more desirable, but God shows us that it is His integrity that He wants us to believe in more than anything else. Yet I believe we have not seen the miraculous on the scale that I am prophesying here. I am prepared to prophesy that there will be miracles that none can gainsay, none can dispute, and none can resist.

"Consequently, faith comes from hearing the message, and the message is heard through the word of Christ" (Rom. 10:17). We are going to have to have a lot of maintenance until we see the last-day ministry. In the meantime, hearing is more important than seeing. "He that hath ears..." We'd better do a lot of listening and have our ears tuned into everything God is saying until He shows His power.

We will be kept from experiencing the power as I am presenting it now unless we remember two things: God is more interested in the upholding of His Word until we meet the criteria for the demonstration of His power. We can either set this back or we can move forward into a glorious last-day revival. God wants to give us more than the tokens of revival that were prophesied in October 1990.

God is going to give us more than tokens if we continue to honor His Word by believing it, honor the Holy Spirit by obeying Him, and honor the blood of Jesus by trusting Him.

We must not allow the Word of God to be replaced or upstaged by anything, including the prophetic things that we are saying here. It is God's Word that will be fulfilled when God clears His holy name.

Other books by R. T. Kendall:

God Meant It for Good

The God of the Bible

Meekness and Majesty

When God Says "Well Done!"

The Gift of Giving

Calvin and English Calvinism to 1647

Believing God

Jonah

Higher Ground

Your Walk With God Can Be Even Deeper...

With *Charisma* magazine, you'll be informed and inspired by the features and stories about what the Holy Spirit is doing in the lives of believers today.

Each issue:

- Brings you exclusive world-wide reports to rejoice over.
- Keeps you informed on the latest news from a Christian perspective.
- Includes miracle-filled testimonies to build your faith.
- Gives you access to relevant teaching and exhortation from the most respected Christian leaders of our day.

**Call 1-800-829-3346 for 3 FREE issues
Offer #88ACHB**

If you like what you see, then pay the invoice of $21.97 **(saving over $25 off the cover price)** and receive 9 more issues (12 in all). Otherwise, write "cancel" on the invoice, return it, and owe nothing.

Charisma Offer #88ACHB
P.O. Box 420626
Palm Coast, FL 32142-0626

Experience the Power of Spirit-Led Living